FAITH
AND
FREE THROWS

*Seven Days to Improve Your Game
And Your Life*

J. L. JEFFERSON

Unless otherwise indicated, all Scripture references are taken from the King James Version of the Bible. Copyright © 1979, 1980, 1982 by Thomas Nelson, Inc. Used by permission. All rights reserved.

Faith and Free Throws *Seven Days to Improve your Game and Your Life*
Written by J. L. Jefferson
Copyright © 2017 by J. L. Jefferson. All rights reserved.

This book may not be reproduced, transmitted, or stored in whole or in part by any means, including graphic, electronic, or mechanical means without the express written consent of the author except in the case of brief quotations embodied in critical articles and reviews.

Dedication

For John Samples, Coach Alex Gillum, Dewayne Scales, Steve Johnson, Julius "Dr. J" Irving, Keith Jefferson (my little brother), Carey Neal, Dennis "The Worm" Rodman, C.J Miles, and my Heavenly Father who were my primary motivators in developing my great love for the game of basketball.

Forward

This book will take you on an awesome spiritual, as well as a physical excursion. It will challenge the reader to examine the core essence of true spiritual power within; using basketball as a visual and tangible tool. It is a user-friendly book that harmoniously illustrates succinct comparisons between act of fundamentally shooting a free throw in the game of basketball and the ability to simply believe and accept the free gift of salvation from God through Christ the creator of our world. Explore an insightful study of the Holy Bible through basketball. We will examine issues pertaining to leadership, fellowship, and stewardship, as it relates to our analogy of simply shooting a basketball in a hoop.

Other topics include, but or not limited to Christian Discipline, The Renovation of the Heart and Mind, hope, imagination, the physical human body and how these topics compare with shooting the basketball with accuracy, proficiency, and God's covenant to man of blessed assurance. This book takes a glimpse from the eyes of a young man who unlike most of the basketball players on his high school team; was first introduced to the game when he was an eleventh grader. Our author, *J. L. Jefferson* has selected an excellently descriptive title: *"Faith and Free Throws"* It is the literal doctrine that presents an outstanding array of basketball and biblical truths.

To begin, as a young boy growing up in the city of Dallas, Texas in the early 60's and 70's, Jefferson grew up in the inner city where there were no assessable basketball courts or recreation centers or YMCA's located in the neighborhood. There were only a few kids in the neighborhood that had basketball goals in the yard. There was one option in my neighborhood when we played basketball and we used the dirt from the ground as our court.

It may sound humorous, but there were actually some benefits to learning how to play the game in the dirt first.

For instance, you are forced to learn how to dribble the ball with control, since the goal is hanging on maybe a tree or the side of your house; it might not be exactly 10 ft as the official height should be. This means you will have to learn how to adjust your game and shoot the ball to hit the part of the rim, so it would bounce from that angle, and hit the inner side of the net. However, with the good, there have to be some bad or negative aspects to playing the game in the dirt. For instance, there was no half court, no full court, no calls, no out of bounds, and absolutely no free throws.

That's right if you really wanted to play basketball where I grew up... (*And I did*), you would play in the dirt and like it! With this descriptive introduction to the game, there is no wonder that I didn't really learn how to play organized basketball on the court until high school. Once I discovered the game on the official level with rules, structure, and running plays; needless too say, I was completely lost. From a religious perspective, it was like the Creation period of our world.

Originally, Adam was in Paradise, or what he understood was Paradise, because he really had nothing else to compare it to. *Why was it Paradise?* I think it was because he understood it, this was his normal. Just like playing in the dirt was my normal. Like Adam's world, I was free to walk around in the dirt without rules and without regulations. If I needed a free throw line, we simply got a stick and drew one in the dirt. There was only one tree that God warned Adam and Eve not to eat from or they would surely die, and they challenged His authority and instantly introduced death into both theirs and our world.

As we carefully examine the attributes of both worlds; the world without bounds and limits and the world with laws, rules, and regulations.

There are common denominators that we can observe which would introduce a myriad of parallels. Consider the magnificent precision, the intricate detail, and spiritual self-control manifested from a *"world without form and void."* According to Scripture, this was our world from the beginning. Simultaneously, in the beginning, that is, during Creation; then the **word** of God was spoken. Certainly, we know the word was with us from the beginning because the word was God in Spirit. *Enjoy!*

Preface

In 1891, Dr. James Naismith is credited as the inventor of the game of basketball. The general idea was to assemble a team of ten players on the court to compete for approximately four, twelve minute quarters. The objective is to have each team compete against the other and to attempt shooting the basketball in the basket before the end of each quarter. Each basket scored would represent two points for the team. The team with the most points scored by the end of the forth quarter wins the ball game! Obviously, there were rules established to allow the opposing team to defend their goal and prevent the player from making the shot. Initially, the task proved to be quite daunting because the entertaining portion of the game is when the player scores a basket. However, in the early days, the basketball players were pretty good at shooting the ball as long as they were "open" and free to shoot. This "opened the doors" pardon the pun; for coaching strategy that would ultimately be designed to leave the offensive player open and able to score. Also, because the original players were hardly scoring and frequently fouled; this led to the introduction of the infamous foul shot or free-throw. At that time, the free-throw shot was usually made up for more than half of the total points scored. Today, we have All-Star players such as Shaquille O'Neal and Dwight Howard, with absolutely horrible free-throw shooting percentages. With that introduction to the game, may I present ***"Faith and Free Throws: Seven Days to Improve Your Game and Your Life"***.

Purpose of the Text

The primary objective in writing the book is two-fold. I hope to utilize the avenue of combining the popular sport of basketball to be used as a catalyst to introduce Christian fundamentals, principals, and values while simultaneously teaching the art of accurate free-throw shooting. Additionally, the purpose is to attempt to make a major impact in the game of basketball.

As Christians, we are all called to ministry. The Bible refers to this ministry of the believer as **The Great Commission**. In short, our mission is simply to lead the lost to Christ. In a recent profile analysis of the high school, college, and professional basketball players in America; we have identified specific common denominators. For instance, he/she is typically tall, minority multi-cultural, with strong leadership characteristics.

According to Scripture, **"Whom He did predestinate, them he also called: and whom he called, them he also justified, and whom he justified, them he also glorified"** (Romans 8:30). Our reasonable service is to present our bodies to God as a living sacrifice for His purpose (Romans 12:1).

FAITH
AND
FREE THROWS

*Seven Days to Improve Your Game
And Your Life*

J. L. JEFFERSON

Table of Contents

Dedication iii
Forward v
Preface .... - 8 -
Purpose of the Text 9

Part 1
THE FOUNDATION

CHAPTER 1
Establishing Proper Basketball Form 18
    Scriptural Analogies and Parallels 19
    Contemporary Context 20
    Form Drills Day 1 20
    Statistical Context 21

CHAPTER 2
Hope and Imagination in the Game of Basketball 23
    Drills and Exercises: Day 2 24
    Scriptural Analogies and Parallels: 24
    Theoretical Explanations 28
    Gillum-ISM's Quote Interpretation No.2 33

CHAPTER 3
Building On a Healthy Foundation 34
    Scriptural Analogies and Parallels 35
    Drills and Exercises: Day 3 35
    Exercising Your Basketball Faith 35
    Practice Makes Perfect 43
    Christian Discipline Summary 46

Drills and Exercises: Day 4 47
Gillum-Osophie's Quote Interpretation No.3 48

CHAPTER 4
Framing Your Game With Your Words 49
    Scriptural Analogies and Parallels 50
    Basketball Power of the Tongue 51
    Understanding the Rules of the Game 52
    Drills and Exercise: Day 5 53
    Gillum-ISM's Quote Interpretation No.4 53

Part 2
GENERAL PROFICIENCIES

CHAPTER 5
The Free-throw Ritual 55
    Mathematical Concepts, Profiles, and Percentages 55
    Development, Leadership, and Implementation 56
    Drills and Exercise: Day 6 61
    Gillum-ISM's Quote Interpretation No.5 61

CHAPTER 6
Timing, Rhythm, and Motion 63
    Free Throw Rudiments and Melodic Elements of the Game ... 63
    Quality Control 64
    Drills and Exercises: Day 7 65
    Gillum-ISM's Quote Interpretation No.6 65

CHAPTER 7
Concentrate On the Target 66
    Eyes on the Prize 68
    Biblical Perspective 69
    Day 7 Drills and Exercises 74

Gillum-ISM's Quote Interpretation No.7.................................74

CHAPTER 8
Three Seconds..76

CHAPTER 9
Diligently... 81
    Crowns of God 81
    Crown of Knowledge 82
    Crown of Life...82
    Crown of Rejoicing 82
    Crown of Righteousness 83
    Crown of Glory and Honour (The crown of Jesus)....83
    Crown of the Conqueror..83
    Crown of Wisdom..84
    Crown of Lovingkindness and Mercy 84
    Crown of Pride (You do not want to receive) 84
    Crown of Old Men 84
    crown of the anointing oil of God............................84
    Crown of Thorns (You do not want to receive).......85
    Diligently Seeking the Kingdom: 85

Summary... 89
    Top 12 Spiritual Gifts Freely Given by God 92

Invitation to Christian Discipleship and Ambassadorship............. 94

CREDITS 95

NOTES 96

Part 1

THE FOUNDATION

CHAPTER 1

Establishing Proper Basketball Form

You will never learn how to shoot a free-throw with any accuracy until you first learn how to establish proper form. As in most everything, there is one exception (*Joakim Noah, Chicago Bulls*) but even he is consistent with his form and therefore reasonably accurate on the free - throw line, he consistently shoots his free-throw with the most obscure form. Which in its own way teaches us that even if the form is considered odd or unusual if you are consistently using the exact same form each time you go to the line; your average will become consistent. This book will teach from a very real coach perspective. My teaching technique is straight-forward but never meant to offend. Therefore, please do not take any comments personally. I am positive that there will be nothing said that has not been said before; probably by your training coach. Perhaps, only stated or taught in a different way.

With that disclaimer, let's use Mr. Noah's free throw as an example in this lesson. I believe it is probably the ugliest free-throw in the NBA. I really don't understand how in the world he makes a single shot with that form. I am completely shocked every time his shot goes threw the hoop. Here is my best assessment; the common denominator is he shoots the ball exactly the same way every time.

Sounds simple, doesn't it? Actually, it takes lots of continuous practice shooting the ball the same way every time in order to master *your* particular form. In my workout sessions, I have my guys stand just inside of the circle located in front of the free-throw line. Although they are now closer to the basketball goal, you may think this would make the task of making a consistent shot even easier, *Right?*

Remember the objective is to establish a form that you are comfortable shooting with. Afterward, we focus on percentages. Now take ten shots using your form the exact same way each time you shoot. Keep a count on how many you hit and missed out of ten. Repeat this process nine more times and after your first hundred shots, you should have an established form. Repeat this exercise daily.

Note: ***Be sure to have some assistance when you practice. You should not move from the free-throw line, have your partner to pass the balls back to you and monitor your average after each shot.***

Scriptural Analogies and Parallels

Believe it or not, there are some excellent values to be learned in the concept of following instructions. To follow instructions requires a certain measure of faith in the person you are receiving the information or direction from. In other words, you are walking by faith and not by sight. (2 Corinthians 5:7). I use this analogy because when you go through the exercise to establish your basketball form you will probably be a little discouraged on your first 100 attempts and the fact that you have missed so many shots. The fact is you never really took the time to actually count your hits and misses. Now, be honest with yourself in answering this question. *"Do you really believe you would have made more or fewer shots because you could see them going in or because you were keeping a written tally?"*

Allow me to answer; it would not have made any difference because you would be shooting the basketball exactly the same way. For instance, if you shoot from your shoulder sometimes and from the wrist other times; your percentage scores will be inconsistent. When you have the opportunity to actually witness with your own eyes the level of consistency you are achieving, your confidence, as well as faith, grows stronger or weaker based on the results. But faith without works is dead. **"For as the body without the spirit is dead, so faith without works is dead also"** (James 2:26).

Contemporary Context

In the story of Noah's Ark, he is challenged to walk out on faith to meet a task that he is unfamiliar with. He is given instructions with precise measurements to build the ark for a reason that he couldn't relate too at the time? Think about it, there was no record of any prior history of rain. *Why do we need an Ark?* For that matter *what is an Ark?* This was truly blind faith, or as previously mentioned, walking by faith and not by sight. This is what is required in this exercise. The faith of Noah may sound impossible, but Scripture teaches us that it only takes faith the size of a mustard seed together with His faith to accomplish any deed.

Form Drills Day 1

First, raise your hands high like you were being robbed. Next use you're shooting arm and point the elbow, bent slightly in the direction of the basketball rim. While establishing your form we need to raise the level and reach of your game. Using only your fingertips while handling the ball, take one hand for balance and the other is cocked backward in a cup like motion, now handle the ball with your fingertips shoot and release.

Statistical Context

Today, LeBron James is recognized as the undisputed best basketball player in the NBA. He is absolutely built for the game. His physical physique is devastating; his leaping ability is in the OZONE... His shooting skills are exceptional. He handles the basketball with the talent and speed of a small guard, and he is nearly 350 pounds, 6 feet 9 inches tall.

As a matter of fact, he is the first player to enter the game of professional basketball with a 90 million dollar contract from a sponsor before he had ever even shot his first basket in the NBA. Let's take a look at some of his statistics and see if we can determine why he was predicted to excel so high by the experts. Not only was he a gifted athlete, superior amongst his competitors in basketball, he was just as talented in the game of football. Never has the NBA offered accolades to an unproven talent like this. To date, he has won two championships and on target to perhaps win a third in the coming season. Is he everything the experts predicted? Absolutely *UHHUH!* In a recent mathematical study conducted by *Khan Academy, LeBron James,* and the *Khan Academy* examined his approach to free throws and concluded with a numerical phenomenon. We will look at this in more detail in later chapters.

"Know Your Personnel"

— Gillum-ISM's Quote Interpretation No.1:

Coach Alex Gillum (1937-2014) was my high school basketball coach. He is the man whom I personally credit for helping me to develop and establish my love for the game of basketball. In our daily practice sessions after school, Big Gil, aka Coach Gillum would motivate us with his "words of wisdom." I lovingly refer to these quotes from my high school basketball coach as Gillum-osophie's. Enjoy.

In this quote, the coach is specifically dealing with on-the-court play. He always stressed in our daily practice sessions that we should practice and maintain good court vision.

> "Remember, when you have possession of the basketball, you have full control of the game. If, and when you should decide to pass the ball to another team player, you have just relinquished control of the game to that player. It is an important decision each and every time. The choice you make may very well determine the overall outcome and make the difference whether or not your team wins or loses the game. In these cases, it is crucial for the player to remember this quote. If you pass the ball to a player for an open jump shot and you already know he is not a very good shooter, you should not pass him the ball. However, if you know and understand the strengths and weaknesses of each of your four teammates on the court, you will always make the right decision."

—*Coach Alex Gillum*

CHAPTER 2

Hope and Imagination in the Game of Basketball

To attempt a free-throw shot without hope and/or imagination is like shooting dice or playing the slot machines in Las Vegas. There is a *chance* you could make the shot. If you have a decent shot, the chances are greater that you will probably make the next shot. However, according to Scripture, "without vision, the people perish". *Too preachy?* OK, let's reverse this concept; when we attempt a free-throw using hope and imagination, the element of chance is dissipated. Does this mean I will never miss another free-throw? No, but your shooting percentage will be so greatly improved that it will appear to onlookers as if you never miss. In this chapter we will examine the intricate spiritual, mental, and physical aspects involving the evolution of the perfect free-throw, using the mind. In the last chapter, we looked at how to shoot the basketball with the correct form. This involves an action on the part of the player. However, before this action is performed, let's consider some common denominators leading up to the point of action. First of all, unlike any other time in the game of basketball; when we shoot the free-throw, the time and motion of the game have to cease. Another important point is there is no opponent attempting to hinder the shooter at the free-throw line. Finally, this is the only time in the game where the players are in a word allowed an opportunity to use the mind and concentrate, focus, meditate on the target. The last point, as opposed to one attempt at the basket at a time, in this portion of the game the player is given two or three consecutive chances to freely shoot the basketball.

When you step back and really think about it, the question that comes to mind is why do we have so many players missing so many free-throws?

Drills and Exercises: Day 2

For this chapter, I recommend you find a gymnasium and we will work on cardio. That's right, Suicides! For those who have experienced this drill, you already understand this works better under the direction of a good training coach. You simply run full speed to the half court line, then back, then full speed to the other end of the court. Repeat at least 25 times.

Scriptural Analogies and Parallels:

"I say to you today my friends, that in spite of the difficulties and frustrations of the moment... I still have a dream! It is a dream deeply rooted in the American dream. I have a dream that one day this nation will rise up and live out the true meaning of its creed: 'We hold these truths to be self –evident: that all men are created equal... I have a dream today." This was a speech delivered on August 28, 1963, by Dr. Martin Luther King Jr. In this most eloquent speech, we could replace the words dream with imagination and or hope without losing any of the significant literal quality or substance. His personal dream became the visionary quest of a nation. It serves as an excellent platform to illustrate the human attribute, ability, or gift which God has given us through our dreams, thoughts, and imagination.

The structure of the individual authors in Scripture reflects a chronological transition and evolution that is consistent with regards to the subject of man's spiritual imagination and hope. For instance, if I say the word bird, cat, dog, or dinosaur, what do you see? Why do we see a picture in our mind instead of the actual letters? We are instinctive, naturally, and superbly created this way. According to Scripture, **"And God said, 'Let us make man in our image..."** (Genesis 1:26).

The common denominators are obvious in creation; God has chosen to make man in his image, but first, he speaks the words and the image appears in his mind. Also, based on the fact that we are all capable of activating an image in our minds; we have the same ability to use this experiment of suggestion in others.

The question then becomes, *"Is this awesome and powerful tool a gift from God or a curse?"* If a gift, why do so few of us know about or utilize this power to our advantages? This is to suggest that of the sixty-three times the word "imagination" is used in the Bible, it is only used once in a positive sense.

Throughout the Scriptures, these inspired writers create, as well as demonstrate important and thematic illustrations on the powerful imaginations that men possess. For example, Noah's Ark and the Tower of Babel provided persuasive evidence of both man's individual and unified ability to utilize spiritual imagination and hope to achieve greatness. Chronological history teaches us how this source of power could be used in unity. This presents an interesting conundrum. How could Noah even imagine an ark? According to Scripture, God gave specific instructions pertaining to the construction of the ark.

In fact, it was the wickedness of man's imagination that prompted God to command the building of the Ark. **"And God saw that the wickedness of man was great in the earth and that every imagination of the thoughts of his heart was only evil continually"** *(Genesis 6:5)*. If we go back to our experiment, we can then begin to understand how the limitations of our imagination and the ability to influence or be influenced by another could be used for good or evil deeds. In our other scenario, the Tower of

Babel very craftfully presents complimentary parallels, threads, and stages to subtly introduce the enormous power of man's imagination and hope, while working together. ***"And the Lord said, Behold, the people is one, and they have all one language; and this they begin to do: and now nothing will be restrained from them, which they have imagined to do"*** *(Genesis 11:6).*

The parallel between Dr. Martin Luther King's ability to influence and captivate an audience simply through suggestion and that of those who built the Tower of Babel are similar. Both were influenced by suggestion, both would achieve greatness, and both were motivated by the power of their inner visionary ability to hope and imagine. In fact, in the Tower of Babel incident; was the first time on record that because of the imaginations of the people, God decided to scatter the people. He stated there is nothing that they could not do that they imagined. This is amazing! Of course in the March on Washington headed by Dr. King, he would choose to walk in compliance with the Lord. His vision for a nation where all people would be treated with equal justice and freedom would become infectious.

It would inspire those in attendance as well as those who would hear his words later. The parallel is also consistent with that of the creation of the world. Everything that God created in those six days, He spoke into existence first. Consequently, the writer has set in motion a chronological pattern that evolves throughout the Bible.

There is a precise continuity with speaking the things we imagine into existence. If I should say the words big yellow bird, or tiny short haired cat, or even big red dog, what image comes to mind? In your mind's eye, you can actually see or imagine both the color and size of the objects that I have suggested. Thus, I have assumed control of your thoughts. Can you imagine how the improper use of this inherited attribute could be used to destroy? My position is likened to that of Paul Revere; the town crier. I literally want to run out into the streets and tell everyone about this! I believe the ability to imagine and hope is also a tremendous responsibility and certainly an underutilized resource that God has given us. I can imagine Adam, the first man in the garden with Eve and ask the question: *"Why did God place this forbidden tree in the middle of such a beautiful garden?"* I believe He chose to make us free will creatures. His desire is that we would and should choose to obey His will. However, the announcement like the Garden of Eden would have to come with a warning.

We should be aware that the inherited ability to imagine and hope is a great gift. If we are not carefully monitoring our thoughts, imaginations, and hopes, it could be used as a weapon of mass destruction by Satan. **"Casting down imaginations, and every high thing that exalted itself against the knowledge of God, and bringing into captivity every thought to the obedience of Christ"** (2 Corinthians. 10:5). Television, radio, newspapers, magazines, and even the internet are some of the tools used today that may alter our thoughts and imaginations on a particular subject. For example, you may be researching a particular subject on the internet, and suddenly an advertisement with a scantily dressed young lady, holding in her hands the product she is promoting. This becomes a distraction and your imagination begins to wonder. The orchestrations of your actions begin with you and the inherited right of choice that God gave us.

Ultimately, the imaginative power is in our hands. Our only limits are based upon our personal visions, hope, and spiritual imagination. According to Andrew Wommack, theologian, author, and scholar, the story of David and Goliath came alive for him when he exercised imagery. He actually marked off nine feet on a tree, because the Bible teaches us that this was Goliath's height. Then he would mark off about five feet to establish the height of David. This exercise helped him to truly visualize and opened the doors of his imagination to vivid detail and conception. There is also an existential philosophy of hope and imagination that we must explore. *"For we are saved by hope: but hope that is not seen is not hope: for what a man seeth, why doth he yet hope for" (Romans 8:24)?* The concept of life existing after death requires thought and perception.

"What do you really think about near-death experiences?" Zaleski replies, *"What I really think... is that the God of Abraham, Isaac, and Jacob is at once a God who declares, "No one shall see me and live," and a God who wishes to be known."*

To illuminate her argument on behalf of religious imagination, she asks, "If God is willing to descend into our human condition (the Incarnation), may not he also, by the same courtesy, descend into our cultural forms and become mediated to us in them and through them?"

Hope is your imagination and faith is the substance of things hoped for. Your imagination is where we conceive things. Human existence is dependent upon hope and imagination. Your imagination is the process of seeing something that you can't see with your eyes. Hope is using the same process. *"Because that, when they knew God, neither were thankful; but became vain in their imaginations, and their foolish heart was darkened" (Romans 1:21).*

Theoretical Explanations

We must practice meditating on a thing until we can see them. As an elementary basketball player/coach, I teach a player how to shoot a free throw by standing at the line, closing your eyes and before you shoot, you must see the ball going through the basket and through the net. *"As a man thinks in his heart, so is he" (Proverbs 1:23).* There is also an eschatology theory of hope and imagination that examines the future, not just the future, the new age. If we are to imagine an eternity with lakes of fire and brimstone or heavens with harps and golden streets and angels the undeniable fact about the future of every person is the inevitability of death. We are then to imagine seeing the face of God or Satan. The Scriptures is clear on this subject. God, our Good Shepherd, does not desire to lose any of His sheep to evil. **No, not one!** Unfortunately, it is also an undeniable fact that many will be lost.

Patience and hope are where your imagination is linked. Hope provides the motivation for your faith. The Scriptures teach us the things that we are to think on or meditate on. *"**Finally, brethren, whatsoever things are true, whatsoever things are honest, whatsoever things are just, whatsoever things are pure, whatsoever things are lovely, whatsoever things are of good report; if there be any virtue, and if there be any praise, think on these things**" (Philippians 4:8).* This is not a suggestion made by God, but a commandment. In order to fulfill this ordinance, it is a Holy prerequisite that we are to use our imaginations to full capacity.

When we think on the things that are just, pure, lovely, virtuous, of good report, of praise...my mind leads me to His Word. It is the only thing that I can imagine that meets these very specific criteria. I am reminded of the story of Joshua; after Moses had died and a new leader had to be named. God spoke to Joshua. He assured him that as he was with Moses, so shall he be with him.

He then commanded him to be strong and very courageous and to meditate day and night upon His word. *"**This book of the law shall not depart out of thy mouth; but thou shalt meditate there day and night, that thou mayest observe to do according to all that is written therein, for then thou shalt make thy way prosperous, and then thou shalt have good success**" (Joshua 1:8).* The subject of imagination is to seek to please God in obedience; the hope is to obtain glory by aspiring to live in the land of milk and honey; a Utopia or heaven on earth. This is consistent with all aspects of my report. Throughout our historical and biblical records; we can document chronologically how God has presented thematic scenarios in which man has either been glorified or consumed by hopes and imagination. *"While we look not at the things which are seen, but at things which are not seen: for the things which are seen are temporal; but the things which are not seen are eternal"* (2 Corinthians .4:18).

There is power to heal and rise from the dead in our hope and imagination. Before our Lord and Savior, Jesus Christ would come; John the Baptist would prophesy. He would identify himself as a voice in the wilderness. His message was to tell everyone of His vision of a Savior to come.

He was a man of great hope and imagination. According to Scripture, even Jesus Christ declared he was more than a prophet... **"Verily I say unto you, among them that are born of women there hath not risen a greater than John the Baptist: notwithstanding he that is least in the kingdom of heaven is greater than he"** *(Matthew 11:11)*. This is a phenomenal statement because this would include quite an impressive list of people who have lived and died, such as Abraham, Elijah, Joseph, Job, Moses, Noah, and even David but also he included, even the least in Heaven.

This same man while in prison doubted the Lord. He sent a messenger to ask Jesus once more; are you the Christ, or should we look for another? Jesus, after allowing John the Baptist's messenger to witness Him in his ministry simply reminded him by saying... Go and show John what you have *seen* and heard... **"The blind receive their sight and the lame walk, the lepers are cleansed, and the deaf hear, the dead are raised up, and the poor have the gospel preached to them"** *(Matthew 11:5)*. The apostle Paul said it this way... **"We walk by faith, and not by sight."** *(2 Corinthians 5:7)*. Jesus is the Lord of both the world of the visible and invisible. If you are blind, through your spiritual imagination, you can see Him. If you are deaf, you will hear His voice.

"For by him were all things created, that are in heaven, and that are in earth, visible and invisible, whether they be thrones, or dominions, or principalities, or powers: all things were created by him, and for him:" (Colossians 1:16). Of course, there is sickness, death, and even mental illness that we must battle today. According to the philosopher, theologian William F. Lynch, he argues that the mentally ill person is he who does not possess imagination... Confusion is a part of existence, but amid the confusion, man must have hope... The mentally ill person is one who is hopeless amid the confused world, and because he lacks imagination and cannot wish, he is left only to fantasize... Lynch states that fantasy fails to live in the world of facts, truth, and reality.

There is salvation in our hope and imagination. *"For in that he died, he died unto sin once: but in that he liveth unto God. Likewise reckon ye also yourselves to be dead indeed unto sin, but alive unto God through Jesus Christ our Lord"* (Romans 6:10-11). Now, this exercise will certainly test your hope and imagination skills. We are commanded to imagine ourselves as dead, just as Christ died for our sins.

That part of your carnal body that desires to commit adultery, use drugs or over indulge; we must put it on the same cross that Jesus was nailed and crucify it to death. Using that same imagination we are to see ourselves resurrected with Christ.

"For if we have been planted together in the likeness of his death, we shall be also in the likeness of his resurrection" (Romans 6:5).

Additionally, the inspired writers of Scripture have presented contrast, and parallels as well as the effective use of symbolism. For instance, the emphasis is used frequently upon hearing and seeing, understanding the reader would relate to the things that are tangible. The Bible and the symbolic use of the blood of Jesus, the Cross, the grave, the old man and the new man are often times presented in parable form. The parable is a concept used by Jesus Christ in most of His sermons which used the natural things of life to illustrate and explain the spiritual. Historically understood, Christ's atonement gives *hope* to Christians in their sin and in their suffering. If we have any assurance of *salvation*, it is because of Christ's Atonement; if any joy, it flows from Christ's work on the Cross. The Atonement protects us from our natural tendency to replace religion with morality and God's grace with legalism. Apart from Christ's atoning work, we would be forever guilty, ashamed, and condemned before God."

> *"It is much better to be thought a fool,*
> *Than to speak and remove all doubt."*

—Coach Alex Gillum

Gillum-ISM's Quote Interpretation No.2

"In this quote, the coach is emphasizing the fact that many times we can use faulty judgment while in the game. He would often test us with questions where we would be required to use reasonable judgment based upon proven results. He would then present a real life game scenario and ask us to explain what we would do in this case, and why? These scenarios would many times prove to be embarrassing because sometimes teammates would make obviously terrible decisions and give totally ridiculous explanations. It is in these times that the coach would take the opportunity to 'rub it in' and use this quote. Although embarrassing, the results were certainly effective because we would think twice before giving a silly answer. It would also train us to always practice utilizing critical and reasonable thinking while in the game."

—Coach Alex Gillum

CHAPTER 3

Building On a Healthy Foundation

This is perhaps the most primary role of a good steward. It is absolutely essential to the athlete that he/she must take good care of their body. Otherwise, all of the prior discussion from our earlier chapters is of no use. You could practice shooting your free-throw, using the very best form, with the power of suggestion utilizing the hope and imagination of John F. Kennedy... If you don't build on a healthy foundation, your efforts will all be in vain. Many of you have probably already realized this is an excellent segue to introduce the element of faith. *"Moreover it is required in stewards that a man is found faithful"* (1 Corinthians 4:2).

According to Scripture, the care of our body is not to be taken lightly. We have a responsibility, a requirement, in fact, a commandment from God; *"I beseech you, therefore, brethren, by the mercies of God, that ye present your bodies a living sacrifice, holy, acceptable unto God, which is your reasonable service"* (Romans 12:1). As a basketball player and coach, I have always placed emphasis on the fact that my team will not run out of gas because of poor work ethics. My high school basketball coach uses to refer to us as "running horses." Certainly, if you have played the game for any length of time, you have personally witnessed as I have while playing the opposing team which for the first two or three quarters were really making life hard for you on the floor. By the second half or third quarter, the crowd in the stands may not see it but you can hear the guy you're defending breathing hard. In this case, although the team may be fundamentally more talented than your team; if they are not operating under this most reasonable standard, they will lose the game every time.

Scriptural Analogies and Parallels

Drills and Exercises: Day 3

This chapter I need you to stretch your ligaments. Actually, it is a good practice and I highly recommend stretching exercises before each practice and before each game. Give yourself at least a good 10-12 minutes stretch. I suggest enough to warm up the body and prepare it for some strenuous activity.

Exercising Your Basketball Faith

Every new believer must first understand that the cornerstone of Christianity is **faith**. This statement is based upon five primary principles. First of all, in order to serve the kingdom of God, you have to be a living creature. Once you are dead, the opportunity to glorify God and win souls for Christ sake is gone. The first Scripture deals with just that… *"The just shall live by faith"* (Romans 1:17; Habakkuk 2:4; Hebrews 10:38; Galatians 3:11). This statement was such a strong principle that the Scriptures sites four witnesses. Additionally, Scriptures teaches us to *"But if he will not hear thee, then take with thee one or two more, that in the mouth of two or three witnesses every word may be established"* (Matthew 18:16; 2 Corinthians 13:1).

Our next foundational point is based upon *salvation*. In deed as a believer, we have to understand our primary goal as living creatures is to diligently strive to obtain eternal salvation. The bible teaches us *"For by grace are ye saved through faith; and that*

not of yourselves: it is the gift of God" *(Ephesians 2:8)*. This Scripture makes it perfectly clear that God in one majestic move has divinely given us two wonderful gifts: *"Grace"* and *"faith"*. Actually, when you think about it, He manages to squeeze two more gifts; they are *"hope"* and *"salvation"*.

However, He let's us know in His word that you will be unsuccessful in achieving faith without the ingredients of His grace. It is sort of like making a cake, or pie or my favorite banana pudding; you already have all of the necessary ingredients. You have your pudding mix, your vanilla cookies, and your milk, but you can't really make a banana pudding without the bananas... Right?

If that point has not resonated enough for you and you still want to debate the issue. Here is another faith fact that you should consider. The Bible tells us that **"Without faith, it is <u>impossible to please</u> God"** *(Hebrews 11:6)*. Now there is that missing ingredient that I was telling you about. We have already established in Scripture that faith is for the living. This brings up another direct commandment from God... According to the Bible, we have what God describes as a reasonable service regarding our bodies. **"I beseech you, therefore, brethren, by the mercies of God, that ye present your bodies a <u>living sacrifice</u>, holy, acceptable unto God, which is your reasonable service."** *(Romans 12:1)* We who are alive need faith in order to live! Next, we determined that certainly, we need faith to obtain salvation. Also, we established the fact that God describes these necessary things for faith as personal gifts from our Heavenly Father.

At this point, he wants us to receive another extremely valid understanding; simply that you will be unable to truly please God without faith. In our last foundational truth, I used as an analogy the baking of a pie, cake or pudding and the fact that without all of the necessary ingredients we will be unable to make that pudding. Well, this scripture brings that point on home. It places the emphasis on the fact that if you did not understand that, although you may have a pudding without the bananas, without the bananas you will not have a banana pudding. Essentially, He is saying I don't want a strawberry pudding, a peach pudding, or a blueberry pudding. I have already given you the ingredients to prepare a banana pudding. Any other pudding will not please me! The question then becomes obvious... *"Do you want to please God?"*

I will leave the answer to that question open to the reader. The answer should also be quite obvious. **Absolutely**! How do we get faith? The Bible teaches us that ***"Faith cometh by hearing, and hearing by the word of God"*** *(Romans 10:17).* This means we can actually cause faith to come to us, we don't have to go out and get it somewhere like we were shopping at the grocery store or in the mall or something. **Faith comes!** We open our ears to hear from God each time we read His word. Just know faith is on its way! It is like a trail that leads straight to you. All you have to do at that point is to listen, believe and receive it.

What is faith? When I hear this question what immediately comes to mind is a significant clue that lies in the question. What is faith? **Faith is...** meaning faith is always in the present. Why do I say that? According to Scripture ***"Now faith is the substance of things hoped for, the evidence of things not seen"*** *(Hebrews 11:1).*

God could have said faith was, meaning past tense or faith will be, meaning future tense. But no, He said faith is! Also, He begins the verse telling us when; **NOW!** He could have said... faith is now and he would have still remained in context. Another consideration is in our prior analogy which describes faith as an action word. In other words and adverb; he says faith is doing something as opposed to faith will be doing something or faith has done something. The Roman writer said, *"faith comes."* Faith comes to us when we study or listen to His word. In fact, as you read this letter if you listen well, you can actually begin to receive faith. We can dig into this Scripture more and discover many other gospel truths.

This Scripture gives the reader the biblical definition of the word faith. *"**Now faith is the substance of things hoped for, the evidence of things not seen**" (Hebrews 11:1).*

From this sentence, faith is clearly defined as a substance. But what is a substance? Be careful as you continue to read because you will soon see that this is not really talking about your vision. *Why?* Although a substance is tangible, meaning it is that which can be seen with your eyes or even touched with your hands. The writer continues by saying it is the substance of things hoped for and the evidence of things unseen.

But hope is not a substance, hope has no substance. However, when we take hope and add it to our faith, it then gives your hope substance. But what is evidence? It is proof; it substantiates or validates something that you do not have. When we use our five senses, the ability to smell, touch, hear, see, and feel, we are using a natural function to perceive things. However, the things of the spirit of God are not perceived by our senses.

Therefore, this passage is not talking about the things which we can see with our eyes. It is describing what happens when we utilize our spiritual perception after faith has come to us. In short, here is another way that this same Scripture could have been read. Faith is now, the things that I am hoping for, I receive now, the proof that I have received these things is in God's word. By faith, I already have the things that I hope for when I worship and commune with God. The Bible teaches us that **"God is a Spirit: and they that worship him must worship him in spirit and in truth"** *(John 4:24).* You cannot worship the Heavenly Father without faith. We know this because as we have already covered the fact that it is impossible to please God without faith.

Furthermore, the Scriptures admonish us in our understanding that <u>God is the great giver!</u> **"*For I say, through the grace given unto me, to every man that is among you, not to think of himself more highly than he ought to think; but to think*** *soberly, according as God hath dealt to every man the measure of faith"* *(Romans 12:3).* Our Heavenly Father knew in advance what we would all need; **"But my God shall supply all your need according to his riches in glory by Christ Jesus."** *(Philippians 4:19).* The precise amount of faith... (Not a measure of faith, but the measure) for us to live has been pre-measured by the hand of God, to be saved, to be victorious. **"For whatsoever is born of God overcometh the world: and this is <u>the victory that overcometh the world, even our faith</u>**" *(1 John 5:4).* And yes, even to fight! **"Fight the good fight of faith, lay hold on eternal life, whereunto thou art also called, and hast professed a good profession before many witnesses"** *(1Timothy 6:12).*

There is an enormous amount of spiritual food to consume here... For example, have you ever noticed in the Scriptures above pertaining to our need(s) how the Apostle Paul used the word need in a singular as opposed to the plural form? Over the years, I have heard many pastors while preaching from this passage how they always said: **"My God will supply all your needs..."** But the word of God does not need any assistance from us. I believe, and this is my personal opinion, that only an omniscient and omni-present, non-respecter of men, all-knowing God, fore-knew that all we really <u>need</u> is our faith in Him. Obviously, we also need love for God in order to delight ourselves in His word. We need the Holy Spirit living in us serving as our Comforter and we need our Lord and Savior Jesus Christ as our redeemer and propitiator for our sins. It is also understood that we need those fruits of the Spirit found in the book of Galatians. However, none of these things can be received or even comprehended without first obtaining and establishing our faith walk. Remember, the Scriptures teach us to walk by faith **"For we walk by faith, not by sight:"** *(2 Corinthians 5:7).*

More food... <u>God wants us to live life victoriously!</u> **"Nay, in all these things we are more than conquerors through him that loved us"** *(Romans 8:37).* God created us with an innate ability to overcome all kinds of worldly obstacles. For He says, *"**Ye are of God, little children, and have overcome them: because greater is he that is in you than he that is in the world**"* *(1 John 4:4).* Therefore, you can handle the oppression of prison walls, drug addiction, pornography, or any things or anyone who attempts to hold a stronghold in your life. **SIDEBAR:** *(The devil is in this world right now, and according to this Scripture, you are even greater than he is...)* But you must use your faith to fight him. We must stop blaming God for our struggles and calamities that happen in our lives. Begin to think of God as He truly is... **He is the Great Giver!** Remember: *"**The thief cometh not, but for to steal, and to kill, and to destroy: I am come that they might have life and that they might have it more abundantly**"* *(John 10:10).* The very principles of Christianity are based upon this gospel truth.

God is not a thief and God is not a liar. How can you truly live in victory if you do not believe <u>in faith</u> that Jesus Christ, Our Lord, and Savior have already defeated Satan at Calvary for our sakes? *And there is even more...* when we examine our fight we should consider the fact that the good fight of faith is the only time in the bible where we are admonished to fight. Also, keep in mind this is one of the only circumstances where a fight is described as good. A fight is typically thought of as brutal, barbaric, and violent. As a matter of fact, we are not even taught to fight the devil. The word of God tells us to resist the devil, cast out the devil, and even to tread on serpents and scorpions.

When we use our faith to perceive the victory that has already been fought and won by Christ, we realize there is no need to fight the devil... but too fight the good fight of faith. In conclusion, I will leave you with one more nugget. It is an <u>absolute faith must</u>: *"**He that cometh to God <u>must</u> believe that he is and that he is a <u>rewarder</u> of them that diligently seek him**"* *(Hebrews 11:6).* This Scripture remains consistent in our faith infrastructure as it shows us how a sovereign Creator made us in His image as creatures of choice. He could have made us like robots, without a will, completely obedient, and ready to serve His will. However, the absolute and essential faith must say you can always come to God, or you may choose not to come to God; but if you decide to come to Him, you must believe that He is a *rewarder* of those who diligently seek Him.

The spiritual truth lies in your faith and hope in a living, giving, and loving God. Remember, hope and faith are also essential to your diligent search for Christ. One Pastor described hope and faith as the wet in the water. *"You can't get the wet without the water, and you can't have the water without the wet."*

Therefore, you can't get faith without hope and you cannot get hope without faith. This gospel truth affirms the inerrant word of God as a substance that cannot be perceived by our mere senses, but by our spirit. Also, it confirms that God was not speaking of things which we can see with our eyes in *His* definition of faith found in Hebrews 11:1.

When we think of hope we must consider the rudiments of the word. Hope is synonymous with our imagination. We were made in God's very own image, or *imagination* first before we were actual creatures. The worlds were made in *His* imagination also by faith. Keep in mind, the power of our mind; the mind is the only weapon the devil can use to destroy us. He attacks us through our mind. Again, this is the reason we are instructed to fight the good fight of faith. You cannot fight the good fight of faith unless you are a diligent seeker of God's word.

If the only requirement was simply to believe and you will obtain salvation then even the devil would be saved. Did you know the devil believes there is a God? Did you know that the devil also knows Scripture? To receive the rewards of God requires diligent, delightful, and faithful study of God's word. The devil is not willing to make that sacrifice, so he twists, distorts, causes ungodliness towards, perverts, and attempts to confuse the mind.

The Bible teaches us *"For God is not the author of confusion, but of peace, as in all churches of the saints"* (*1Corinthians 14:33*). Since God is the exact opposite of everything that the devil is, it is the devil that uses confusing the mind as his favorite weapon against us. God is a rewarder. Since faith is always in the present tense; we already have the victory, we already have all power, we already have all blessings bestowed upon us, we already have His grace and mercy, and they are actually given to us new every single day. How could a good giving loving God be the cause of devastation in our lives? **He couldn't**. How do we justify tragic events such as earthquakes, bombings, shooting of innocent little children—things that happen in this world; how can you honestly believe God is responsible? **He isn't**.

In fact, there are many contracts that make provisions in the legal document for so called "Acts of God". The implication is clear that one party is not to be held accountable for tragic and unforeseen natural calamities that may happen during the term of the contract.

If we are imprisoned, kidnapped, or placed in any position where we are held against our will and the event may cause injury or even death; we can no longer blame God. These evil acts are and should be understood to be "Acts of Satan". Scripture tells us that he is the thief who comes to steal your life, kill your life, and destroy your life. It further says, I, your God and Creator, have come that you may have *life; and life more abundant* (John: 10-10). How could we confuse the two? They are totally opposite positions. The answer is in our study. Again, I ask you, who is the author of confusion? Who uses your mind thoughts and imagination as a way to manipulate and blind you spiritually? We know from our reading, God has already told us that He is not that author. The answer is Satan the great deceiver. Now God can take an evil and disastrous event from the devil which was meant to destroy and only He can cause good to come out of a horrible situation. According to Scripture, *"But as for you, ye thought evil against me; but God meant it unto good, to bring to pass, as it is this day, to save much people alive" (Genesis 50:20).*

Practice Makes Perfect

A good practice in feeding your spirit begins with a good practice feeding your body. This chapter would not be complete without suggesting some healthy food choices. Although I have never really had what I would refer to as a weight problem, I know many do. Also, I don't really believe in diets. Rather, weight management. For the sake of clarity and time let us begin this discussion from a positive and healthy perspective. Mainly because people who already live at a healthy weight should balance activity and food intake in order to maintain that health range. On the other hand, for overweight people, the goal of weight management is to prevent weight gain, and over time, reduce body fat to a healthy level which can be maintained for a lifetime.

In short, by reducing our food intake, increasing activity, and changing behaviors that contribute to weight gain will help us to achieve our weight management goals. If we were to break the strategies down into steps, the first step would have to be "**assessment**".

This is when we evaluate our current weight, weight history, and existing medical conditions to determine if losing weight is recommended. Also, a person's age is important because extra weight may be less of a health risk at certain times than others. For instance, a teenager still growing, an increase in body weight may be followed by growth spurts that cause his/her BMI to go back into the healthy range. In older adults, a few extra pounds may provide a reserve in the event of long-term illness.

A key factor weather weight loss should be recommended is the presence of diseases or abnormalities that are linked to excess body fat. Such as high blood pressure, sugar, and high blood cholesterol levels, which are all common in overweight people. If someone is overweight and has two or more of these conditions, then weight loss is recommended. There are many factors that contribute to weight problems. Factors like environment, family history, genetics, and metabolism... (which is the way your body changes food and oxygen into pure energy), leads us to our second step... **"energy balance"**.

The amount of energy or calories your body gets from food and drinks (energyIN) is intricately balanced with the energy your body uses for simple things like breathing, digesting, and being physically active (energyOUT) This energyIN/energyOUT theory is an extraordinary strategy as it relates to healthy weight management. To simplify, if you have the same amount of energyIN as you do energyOUT over time equals weight stays the same or (energybalance).

More energyIN than energyOUT equals weight gain. More energyOUT than energyIN equals weight loss. To maintain a healthy weight your energyIN and energyOUT do not have to balance precisely every day. But it is the balance over time that helps to maintain a healthy weight. Our third and final step deals with "**behavioral control or therapy**".

This method evolved from the belief that the feeding behavior of obese people is abnormal and geared towards normalizing their particular feeding behavior or minimizing the consequences of their abnormal behavior. When we look at lean people through the eyes of behavior therapy, they are believed to control their food intake primarily in response to their internal physiological hunger mechanisms while obese people are more responsive to external, non-physiological influences which would result in poor food intake control.

External factors include, but are not limited to things such as the time of day, the palatable food, easy access to food, sight, smell and emotions toward the desired goal of "feeling full" and content. In 2001 the US Surgeon General addressed the rising incidence of obesity by announcing an official government report and call-to-action to "Prevent and Decrease Overweight and Obesity." In this report, he strategically outlined a program designed to encourage and improve food choices and to increase physical activity. "The World Health Organization" projects that by the year 2015 approximately 2.3 billion adults will be overweight.

Also, another 700 million will be obese. In many countries, the incidence of underweight from consumption of too few calories exists as well as being overweight from consuming more calories than expended. With these alarming numbers ever-growing throughout the world, both small countries and large, the issue of strategic weight management is now at epidemic proportions.

My third and final step is "**nutrition transition**". On this platform, we must transition nutrition with economics. Obviously, if the economic condition in a developing country improves, obesity and its accompanying chronic diseases begin to appear. The economic growth will bring better access to food and changes in diet and lifestyle. Although, some of this nutrition transition is positive with shifts in the diet comes increasing life expectancy and decreases in birth-rate, decreases in the incidences of infectious diseases as well as nutrient deficiencies.

Along with the positive, there are always the negative dietary changes in lifestyle that decrease physical activity. With this decrease comes a shift towards less physically demanding occupations, increase in the use of transportation to work or school, more labor saving technology in the home, and more passive leisure time.

This discussion in nutrition is evolving into even greater problems that all appear to stem from changes in diet which affect both over-nutrition and under-nutrition. Because of our nutrition choices and economic infrastructures, the rate in which obesity is increasing demands not only our immediate attention but a committed international strategic plan.

The fact is people are gaining weight because they are eating more and moving less. My prayer is that we all will begin to understand the true value of our holy call to live a healthy lifestyle; that we began to realize our stewardship in the maintenance of our bodies, and that we all will come into compliance with God's command to us for our bodies.

Christian Discipline Summary

To become an effective, productive, and successful force in the game of basketball (as in life), you will have to establish some principles of discipline. The purpose of spiritual discipline is the total transformation of the person. According to Scripture, **"And be not conformed to this world: but be ye transformed by the renewing of your mind, that ye may prove what is that good, and acceptable, and perfect, will of God"** (Romans 12:2).

The mind is renewed by applying it to those things that will transform it. The aim is replacing old destructive habits of thought with new life-giving habits. The first would be the "discipline of study." Study is a specific kind of experience in which through careful attention to reality the mind is enabled to move in a certain direction. We must remember the mind will always take on an order conforming to the order upon which it concentrates.

For the purpose of this topic, we must study our opponent, his strengths, and weaknesses. We must over compensate his strengths and exploit the opponent's weaknesses.

Next, we consider the **<u>discipline of fasting</u>**. Fasting must forever be centered on God. Physical benefits, success in prayer, the enduing with power, spiritual insights—these must never replace God as the center of our fasting. Once the primary purpose has been established, we are at liberty to utilize secondary purposes in our fast. Fasting reminds us that we are sustained by every word that proceeds from the mouth of God (Matthew 4; 4). Food does not sustain us; God sustains us. Therefore, in experiences of fasting, we are not so much abstaining from food as we are feasting on the word of God. *FASTING IS FEASTING!*

Finally, there is the **<u>discipline of service</u>**. In the discipline of service, there is great liberty. It enables us to say no the worldly games of authority and promotion and abolishes our desire or need for "pecking order." How like chickens in the pen, there is no peace until it is clear who is the greatest and who is the least. Or on the basketball court when you and only you are at the free-throw line and the weight of the world appears to be on your shoulders. The point is not to do away with all sense of leadership or authority. Any sociologist would demonstrate the impossibility of such a task. However, we must yield to our own understanding and allocate time for service. It is a mathematical equation that does not compute; the more you give, the more you receive?

<u>Drills and Exercises: Day 4</u>

In this chapter, we will focus the body on reach, extension, endurance, and agility. I need you to give me 4 sets of 25 sides, straddle hops.

"An excuse is like an a##hole; Everybody's got one..."

—Coach Alex Gillum

Gillum-Osophie's Quote Interpretation No.3

This quote deals with the obvious. Coach Gillum trained us to use a hypothesis that will in most cases result in a more positive conclusion. This quote eloquently presents the point that if you need an excuse for anything, there is always one available and any and everyone can make an excuse. I believe he was challenging us to be above the average and press on towards the goal of being someone special on the court and in life.

> *"The fact that we oftentimes make excuses for our mistakes as opposed to owning up to it and admitting the error was an individual mistake. When we own our mistakes on the court and identify the cause; we can better address the problem when it or a similar situation occurs."*

—Coach Alex Gillum

CHAPTER 4

Framing Your Game With Your Words

We have talked about the spiritual, physical, and mental requirements needed to excel on the free-throw line. In this chapter, we will explore the inner power that we all possess when we simply open our mouth and speak. That is correct... tell the ball where you want it to go. This is no magic trick. It is an exercise that must become a ritual practice each and every time you attempt your free-throw shot. Remember, when you shoot you must first use your anointed imagination to visualize the shot going into the basket exactly the way you want it. The process of shooting this free-throw is, in fact, an exercise in faith, prayer, and hope. As the Scriptures admonish; *"Therefore I say unto you, what things soever ye desire, when ye pray, believe that ye receive them, and ye shall have them" (Mark 11:24).*

It is really not just the believing and the hearing, but it is in the "**DO-action**" you take. You must begin to recognize the power to frame your game exactly the way you speak it into creation. *"But be ye doers of the word, and not hearers only, deceiving your own selves" (James 1:22).* Believing in yourself, believing in the shot that you are about to take, telling the ball where to go with your words, and doing all of this simultaneously; knowing that it will happen as you said before it happens is the completion of the exercise in faith. Remember the biblical definition of the word of faith. Faith is always in the present, never in the future. **Faith is now!**

The free-throw is always performed in the present. What am I saying? Make the process of shooting your free-throw a spiritual commune between you and God.

As a Christian man of faith, you should know there are always angels around you faithfully listening for the word of God to be spoken from your mouth. These angels have been dispatched to administer the will of God. God wants us to have the desires of our hearts. This is written in His last will and testament. The catch clause is to make sure your desires are consistent with the will of God. The angels of heaven have no other assignment, but to do the will of God. If you are speaking His will, they will obey. This is not luck, this is not magic. This is blessed assurance and the will of God being delivered. Like all things, the more you begin to practice this exercise process and implement it into your game as your free-throw ritual; you will only get stronger and you will begin to witness your free-throw percentage as it increases.

Scriptural Analogies and Parallels

"And God said..." From the beginning of time, these three words were uttered by our Creator and Heavenly Father. The keynote to remember is that these words like faith were spoken in the present tense. They were also spoken just before the action was performed and then they happened. But, if this was the beginning of everything; who was he speaking too? Was this action recorded for our understanding? According to Scripture; **"In the beginning was the Word, and the Word was with God, and the Word was God"** (John 1:1).

As we frame our world using the example of the creator of the world; consider the possibility that God was speaking to ministering angels whom he relied upon to assist Him with the task that he has commanded to happen. We must also consider the fact that when God created man, He made us in his very own image. Since faith is the substance of things hoped for and the evidence of things not seen. This means God actually created two, or at least more than one world; the world of the visible and invisible. **"For we walk by faith, not by sight"** *(2 Corinthians 5:7).*

If we can accept these gospel truths, that there is a Creator who performed these miraculous tasks; we should be able to accept his word as the undisputed truth and spiritual foundation on which the Christian faith is established. Like our Heavenly Father, we have been made with the same power to create and with the same inherited authority over the angels of the host. Of course, we should realize that this power allows us the opportunity to set in motion our destiny.

Basketball Power of the Tongue

As if you haven't got the message yet... You know, I want you to really meditate on the inner power we possess. When I was a young child, I personally witnessed a horrible incident that would inevitably result in the death of my older sister (who was only ten years old at the time) and would ignite the fuse for a very long and hard grieving period in my family's life. The incident was a house fire which would burn all of our possessions and take the life of my sister. In this brief synopsis, the reader is compelled to sympathize with both the emotions of grief and the inevitable consequence of death.

However, it is my intent to illustrate and define to a better understanding of the process of image, hope, and speaking your world into reality. Although most understand they will all eventually die, no one wants to die! It is the evolution of life itself. The primary emphasis should be stewardship and what we choose to do with the little time that we have to live our lives. The Proverb writer said it this way, **"<u>Death and life</u> are in the power of the tongue: and they that love it shall eat the fruit thereof"** *(Proverbs 18:21).*

It should be prefaced by the fact that the writer is speaking to the believer. With that understanding, there should be hope. God has given the believer power from above to determine our life and our death through love. There is also another key to life and death in this Scripture that must be identified; the things you say with your mouth can either build or destroy.

Therefore, we must be careful to monitor our every word. When we consider that during the time of creation, even the world we live in and every living creature were created only when God spoke them into life. He gave us our best illustration of our inherited power when he made man in his image and likeness. He wanted us to **be** and **do** just as He did. Also, remember when God created the first man (Adam), there was no death.

The man opened the door and introduced death through his own disobedience. This is another illustration of our power to choose life or death. God did warn both Adam and Eve of the consequences that their disobedience would introduce certain death.

Since we serve a Creator who can do all things, except one, <u>He cannot lie</u>; death has become an inevitable part of the process of life. *"A good name is better than precious ointment; and the day of death than the day of one's birth" (Ecclesiastes 1:7).*

Understanding the Rules of the Game

When we really begin to accept the fact that in life, just like the game of basketball itself we are governed by rules and regulations. These rules are established as a principle standard that when practiced will enhance the participants and the onlookers. The fact of the matter is we must have these guidelines in place. **"God so loved the world that he gave his only begotten Son, that whosoever believed would have eternal life"** *(John 3:16).* From the very beginning, He has given us the roadmap to achieving our goals and living in His will. We, as faithful believers should utilize the information that God has provided for us to our advantage. He has supplied our every need. He has given us every advantage. As basketball players, we should identify our natural God given ability and combine those skills with the rules or law of the game.

Drills and Exercise: Day 5

Our chapter 4 daily drills will take us back to the court for some shooting drills. I like this drill because it is competitive and requires you to workout with your teammates. You simply divide the team in half; one half on each corner of the gym. Each will have a basketball and will race to the other end of the court while dribbling the ball full speed to the far corner; the shoot the ball from the corner until you make the basket. After you make the basket return by dribbling full speed back to the other end of the court and give the ball to the next teammate. Repeat procedure until the last man has finished.

Gillum-ISM's Quote Interpretation No.4

> *"FOR REAL"*
>
> —*Coach Alex Gillum*

Whenever 'Big Gil' would use this statement we all knew something amazing has just happened on the court. It was a statement of jubilation which emphasized the actual act. Today, I think of outrageously tremendous moves made by players like Stephen Curry, Kevin Durant, and LeBron James.

Part 2

GENERAL PROFICIENCIES

CHAPTER 5

The Free-throw Ritual

In this chapter, we will examine the consistent elements involved in the act of shooting the perfect free-throw shot every time. To preface this discussion, there is absolutely no particular ritualistic concept that works better than the other. The point is developing a ritualistic signature that is yours and yours alone. **You own it!** It is your formal way of addressing the free-throw line each and every time. Once you have personalized it, you must live or die with it.

Mathematical Concepts, Profiles, and Percentages

In this analogy the *Khan Academy* with the assistance of one of the best basketball players in the world LeBron "King" James asked, "What are the odds of making 10 free throws in a row?" Or in mathematical terminology; determine the probability of making 10 free throws in a row. First, we look at his free-throw career average which is around 75%, and then we would imagine there were a million LeBron James' taking that shot at the same time. This means 75% of them would make that first free throw and 25% would miss the first free throw. However, we are not concerning our selves with the 25% who missed.

Let's look only at 75% of the 75% for our 2nd free throw. Now, a pattern is established... we know 75 % of the 75% will make the free throw in the forth, fifth, sixth and so forth. Let's move on to the tenth free throw shot...

Now we multiply 75% x 75% x 75% ten times or (75%) to the tenth power. The word per cent literally means a hundred. Or you may write this as 75 over 100 which is exactly the same as 0.75 to the 10th power. When we evaluate the probability and round it off to the nearest hundred it would calculate to 0.06 which equals about a 6% percent probability of making 10 free throws in a row.

Now, what is your free throw percentage probability? Are there scenario's where it may be better for the team if you intentionally missed the free throw?

Development, Leadership, and Implementation

As we consider the mathematical equations, percentages, and probabilities we simultaneously begin to develop an increase in our overall shooting average. Although most of us can only hope to shoot 10 free throws and hit all 10 of them; the fact is *LeBron James* is an exception to the rule. However, there are professional ball players with even higher free throw shooting averages. For instance, *Kevin Durant* with the *Oklahoma City Thunder* has an average of around 91%. *Stephen Curry* with the *Golden State Warriors* is currently leading the league with an overwhelming 93.2 percent shooting average. Remember, when calculating using this mathematical theory, we always start with the shooting average of the player.

It's tough to argue with accuracy like that. But it should be noted that the Warriors aren't entirely pleased with Curry's performance at the line because he doesn't get there as often as you'd like from such a great shooter.

"If you're going to lead the league in free-throw shooting, you might as well find a way to get to the line more often," *General Manager Larry Riley* said.

But Curry has gotten to the line only 217 times, a far cry from the league's most-fouled point guards, *Oklahoma City's Russell Westbrook* with a whopping **601 free-throw attempts**, and *Chicago's Derrick Rose* with **519**. "You've got to learn how to get in there and bait the guy to foul you," said *Coach Keith Smart*. "Over time, he'll figure it out. He'll learn the nuances of inviting a player to foul him." Curry said he has started to be more aggressive on his drives this season, and he's learning how to sell calls. He has made 202 free throws, which is two more than he attempted all of last season. Some basketball observers often complain that today's players don't spend enough time working on the fundamentals of free-throw shooting, but getting to the line is a skill that must be practiced, too. Skills don't only manifest themselves when a positive result is achieved a player has to create the opportunity to get that result, too. The common denominator in shooting free-throws with accuracy and rituals are often rhythmically as well as numerically consistent.

Whether it's going around-the-back, rubbing face, blowing kisses or humming some peculiar German pop song, you'd be hard-pressed to find an NBA player who doesn't have his own nonpareil routine at the foul line. The following is a Top 10 list of all the tributes, superstitions and, at times, the outright zaniness of the pro baller formula for success on the charity stripe.

1). **Nick "The Quick" Van Exel** shot a confident .794 at the line during his journeyman career, but some people think that his eventual stripe routine was born out of sheer cockiness. After several years in the league as a noted streak-shooter, Van Exel realized that he was much more comfortable taking a couple steps back from the 15-foot mark and dropping them from 17 to 18 feet. Van Exel was quoted as saying he "just felt more comfortable" at that range, and his stats from '99 to '02 definitely proved his point as he shot well into the 80th percentile.

2.) Left-hand shooter Anthony Mason's ritual wasn't so much in the pre-shot routine as the mid-follow through one.

This guy's shot had so much hesitation you might have thought Will Smith could've starred in a lame romantic comedy about it (i.e. *Hitch*). Mason dribbled a few times, held the ball up in his hands as if to release, then spent the remaining three-to-four seconds with the ball perched and paused like an annoying video game glitch as everyone sat dumbfounded. Okay, the guy shot 71 percent for his career, which isn't bad, but that's not what lands you on this list is it?

3.) Hailing from the superstitious player-friendly *University of Arizona* (just check out *Jason Terry*), **Gilbert Arenas,** close to but probably not the least popular player on this maverick's list, exhibits a successful but peculiar style of free throw shooting. Arenas' custom is to wrap the ball around his waist three times before shooting which he developed as a young player. That has settled his mind enough to knock down 80 percent of his career freebies.

4.) Reggie Miller, who shot 89 percent from the line during his career and is the leading vote-getter for induction into the *2011 Basketball Hall of Fame,* could pretty much shoot free throws with his damn eyes closed. But not before completing his ritualistic patented formula for success at the foul line. First, *Miller* would douse his hands in salt-powder, and then he would press the ball left-handed against his left hip and extend his right hand upward in a shooting motion. Finally, he would take three dribbles and let the ball fly. It's hard to argue when you're nailing nearly nine out of 10 from the stripe. *Yeah, it's Miller Time!*

5.) With a sideways dribble, Richard "Rip" Hamilton put his stamp on the game and an 85 percent career free throw percentage in the record books. Hamilton honed his one-of-a-kind formula while at *UConn*, where he led the Huskies to the 1999 *NCAA Championship*. Over his 12-year NBA career, this NBA Champion has nailed free throw after free throw with the same deadly design. First, Rip takes a deep breath, takes two dribbles in front (one on the side) and lets fly a dagger that has downed foes and teams who thought they were destined for victory.

6.) On the short list of routine tributes, retired Jazz guard Jeff Hornacek is at the top spot. This gunner nailed close to 88 percent for his career, hit 67 freebies in a row at one point and sank a staggering **95 percent** in his final season with Utah. But this incomparable guard's acclaim comes from a simple gesture that now lives on video. Hornacek simply took a few dribbles then rubbed his cheek in tribute to his children before launching his shot. A tribute to your kids? I couldn't think of a better reason for the ball which almost always will be going in.

7.) Of the unrivaled and weird habits of NBA players, Dallas' All-Star forward Dirk Nowitski's on-again, off-again musicality at the line probably has fans of *Baywatch* fairly interested. In his first few years, and continuing infrequently through the present, Nowitzki was known to hum American TV star and German pop music sensation *David Hasselhoff's* tune *"Looking for Freedom"* while preparing to launch from the line. Adoring that hit tune as a kid, the German-born Nowitzki—who shoots .876 for his career with several seasons over 90 percent—has clearly found freedom from bricking foul shots.

8.) Ten-time NBA All-Star and triple double specialist Jason Kidd, whose personal life has taken considerable blows in the past decade, paid tribute to his ex-wife Joumana and his kids Trey, Jason, Miah and Jazelle by blowing a kiss before shooting his foul shots. Now with a new wife and life in tow, Kidd can continue his near 75 percent shooting with a clear conscience.

9.) Karl "The Mailman" Malone gave us two trips to the NBA Finals, *36,928 career points* and plenty of frustration that the NBA didn't institute a nine-second rule on the free throw line. He would take a few dribbles, spin the ball up in the air in front of him a few times, set three or four times while whispering an indecipherable mantra, then, with Mason-nasty hitch, he'd release the ball with nine seconds and change on the clock. *Phew!* Quite honestly, **Malone, who attempted 13,188 free throws and made 9,787** of them spent—according to this writer's arithmetic—close to a day-and-a-half on the foul line. Seriously, do the math.

10.) The Big Dipper lands himself in the top spot on this list because his routine had well, a sense of routine-less-ness. A notably horrid career free throw shooter with a 51 percent average, **Wilt Chamberlain** had many free throw shooting advisers over the course of his 14-year career. He was known to have tried a variation on the hook shot, short dribbling routines, softer follow-throughs, more arch, less arch and even the Barry-esque under-handed variation. One of the more unsubstantiated, but not too implausible charity attempts—probably due more to Chamberlain's Paul Bunyan-like stature on the court—was that Wilt tried, but more likely considered, dunking or laying it in on a few occasions. In fact, this prompted rule changes that stated that a player could not cross the foul line in order to shoot his free shot. But just attempting it! If that's true, and there's no film footage to back it up, the 7'1" 275 lb. Chamberlain would have undoubtedly been the first and only to attempt this feat and for that consideration alone the late great lands himself at the top of this list. (**Top 10 free throw rituals provided by Ronald Martinez/Getty Images).**

In conclusion, this brings up my last point as it relates to this topic. Are there scenarios where the players may choose to intentionally miss the free throw? Case and point... *Its 2.0 seconds left in the game, Cleveland –vs- Houston, the date was Sunday, March 1, 2015, the score is tied and James Hardin is on the line and has just hit his first two shots to make the lead by 3 points; at this point would it be better for the team and more strategic if he chooses to intentionally miss his last shot or should he be more concerned with his personal shooting average and go for the score?*

Drills and Exercise: Day 6

If there is any drill and/or exercise that is, in my opinion, absolutely essential in the game it would be learning the Figure 8.

This drill is often applied throughout each and every game. If you watch closely, you will see the rhythm, timing, and flow of the game will operate based upon this concept. Keep in mind the center point is always where the basketball lives; therefore the players will revolve around the center point.

Gillum-ISM's Quote Interpretation No.5

"He who knows not, and knows he knows not, is a fool. Stay away from him."

—Coach Alex Gillum

This quote deals with the definition of stupidity, according to Coach Alex Gillum. Basically, I believe he was saying; if you don't know, you are simply ignorant about the thing you don't know. You simply need to acquire the knowledge necessary to understand. However, if you don't know and attempt to disguise your ignorance by acting as if you do know. This is a fool. Stay away from this person!

CHAPTER 6

Timing, Rhythm, and Motion

Free Throw Rudiments and Melodic Elements of the Game

In our earlier chapters, we have focused our attention primarily on shooting the ball effectively and accurately. However, when it comes down to it most of our basketball contemporaries would agree that good **defense wins** basketball games. It will create more opportunities to control the game-flow and will allow your team increased attempts at victory over the opponent. We will deal with the subject of quality control in greater detail later in this chapter. It is my opinion that you will never become complete B-baller's without applying and utilizing strong defensive tactics. Now, you may wonder why I chose to emphasize defense in a book with a topic that is based upon shooting the free throw. My reason is consistent with our subject because a strong defensive player, like a strong and accurate shooter, will require excellent timing, rhythm, and motion. Basically, we are trying to minimize the amount of movement and minimize the chances for error. The rhythm and timing **must** be identical every time you shoot the free throw. Our rhythm and timing must be incorporated into both our mental and physical mechanics.

To complete the Pre-Shot Routine, it must be done within three seconds using the following steps:

- Elbow In
- Bend your knees
- Follow through with releasing the ball off the fingertips

As you can see, all three elements are applied with the proper rhythmic rudiments and execution. With practice and patience, you will discover these three essential elements are an integral piece throughout all facets of your game. In short, and in most cases; the team controlling the ball most of the game usually has the most attempts to score a basket. Thus, based upon the theory of mathematics, the odds are more than likely a winning game.

Quality Control

As we have already alluded to in the last chapter, controlling your game will control your destiny. You only have about 8 minutes per quarter to achieve your goal of victory. There are 4 quarters in the game if you control the ball approximately 4 minutes a quarter and your opponent controls the ball 4 minutes per quarter; basically and mathematically you have a 50% chance of winning and so does your opponent. How do we increase those chances? We must incorporate strategic defensive opportunities to create turnovers, draw the foul shots by taking more shots that will offer opportunities to shoot free throws. Remember, when we are shooting foul shots, this is the only time in the game where we still control the ball and the clock is turned off. This is what I refer to as creative and critical quality control opportunities.

As a coach, I have seen this concept work against teams who were even more talented than my team as far as ability. However, they were ineffective in strategy. This is another reason; I like to place an emphasis on my team of "running horses" as I like to refer too. In other words, my team will never loose the game because they were out of shape and physically unable to compete with any team. Quality control is the fundamental attribute which is absolutely essential to the committed ball player for defense as well as offense in the game.

Drills and Exercises: Day 7

In this chapter, I will introduce you to what I like to refer to as my "Rocking chair" drill. I call it the rocking chair because you are located directly under the basketball goal and you actually rock from left to right simply laying the ball up against the backboard into the net; then catch and lay the ball up off the backboard with your left hand. Repeat this procedure until you are in perfect timing, rhythm, and motion (Approximately 20 times).

Gillum-ISM's Quote Interpretation No.6

> *"The key to ignorance is the inability to follow directions."*

—*Coach Alex Gillum*

This quote is particularly important and personally, I feel the analogy applies not only to the game of basketball, but it also is a very tried and proven life lesson. For instance, in life on our daily role of job performance, we are often required to listen, learn, and perform specific tasks that require the innate ability to follow instructions.

CHAPTER 7

Concentrate On the Target

As we continue to explore the concept of mastering the technique required to shoot the free throw shot with precision, I am reminded of the age old bible story of David and Goliath. You remember the young lad who would become known as a giant killer; David who would later reign as King. If you remember, David was instructed to choose five smooth stones and his sling-shot as his weapon. However, there is no record that he would be required to use all five stones. He would only need to focus and concentrate on his target, which coincidentally was the head in order to be successful in his mission. David had prepared himself well. He used his weapon often and developed a comfort level that would allow him to freely use his ability to shoot and hit his target with precision. *"And David put his hand in his bag, and took thence a stone, and slang it, and smote the Philistine in his forehead, that the stone sunk into his forehead; and he fell upon his face to the earth. So David prevailed over the Philistine with a sling and with a stone, and smote the Philistine, and slew him, but there was no sword in the hand of David. Therefore David ran, and stood upon the Philistine, and took his sword, and drew it out of the sheath thereof, and slew him, and cut off his head therewith. And when the Philistines saw their champion was dead, they fled"* (Samuel 17:49-51).

Although the Bible does not record this, using my spiritual imagination I would suggest if it were necessary; the young champion probably could have hit the same target five times based upon his intense concentration, training, and preparation. It is my goal in this chapter to introduce to the reader the importance of utilizing the power of the mind when we use our imagination to concentrate on a target to achieve our ultimate goals of success.

The Holy Bible is filled with stories where imagination, mind control, and effective intense concentration would be used to achieve unlimited success. Case and point, the Tower of Babel was a task that would demonstrate the concept of teamwork and show us how a group of individuals working together in agreement could form an alliance and with concentration, imagination, and faith; they could conquer any task with good success. In fact, it was recorded in the Bible that when God looked down on these people and saw they were unified on this target and about to accomplish their goal of building a tower that would reach heaven; He said when these people work together in agreement they would be able to accomplish any goal using their imagination and concentration.

Actually, when we concentrate on a target we use our imagination to see (*with our hearts eye*) the task completed. We can actually see this goal and witness the task as accomplished. We are in essence meditating on the thing that we want to complete. Historically, we can trace this technique from a biblical perspective as early as the first man and the time of Creation. The Scriptures teach us that God created man in His very own image or imagination. Another consistent formula that He used was the fact that each and every thing he created, He actually spoke into being. For instance, God said everything before it was...

In applying these principles to the game of basketball and perfecting the act of shooting the free-throw with extreme accuracy; we must first close your eyes and imagine or visualize the shot going through the hoop.

Important Footnote: *You cannot attempt the shot until you can actually see the shot going through the HOOP in your mind!* We must speak to the ball and tell it where you want it to go.

Finally, we must shoot the ball with faith and blessed assurance; while simultaneously believing the ball will go through the hoop. Faith without works is dead faith. We want to use our God given inner living faith. That is to say, *the measure of faith* that God has already provided for each and every one of us who believe.

Now, from a point of logistics, this process may appear to be a long and tedious process. However, it is like anything that we practice, the more you do it the easier and faster the process. Naturally, your confidence level will increase each and every time you personally witness the ball going through the hoop. In short, your faith in this technique and your ability to make the shot will also increase. You will literally begin to understand and realize that it really does not require a whole lot of faith, **but it does require faith**.

Eyes on the Prize

I suppose by now you probably realize when at the free-throw line; **you** control the game. It is the only time in the game where you are allowed to freely take your best shot to score a point for the team. Obviously, the prize should be in making the basket, wouldn't you say? At this point, keeping your eye on the prize is essential in ascertaining a successful outcome. As I have mentioned in previous chapters identifying the prize must not be misconstrued. The game clock stops, the offense and defensive team stops, the audience is anxiously waiting on you, and nothing in the game proceeds until you have taken the shot. Before you take the shot; remember to visualize the ball coming through the basket.

Biblical Perspective

From a Scriptural viewpoint, there is a very strong parallel between the seemingly simple task of taking and making a free shot and the biblical narrative or mandate that God has provided a free gift to all in *His* Holy Spirit; which appears to be the simple task of acceptance. The Bible offers to the believer the opportunity to receive ever-lasting salvation through acceptance of Jesus Christ as your Lord and Savior.

The existential covenant between man and God is oftentimes illustrated and recorded in many of the sermons of our Lord Jesus Christ when He walked, talked, suffered, and lived for 33 years here on Earth. I have selected the parable of the seed sower as it best represents and parallels the act and principles of teaching one to shoot a free throw with ultimate accuracy, while simultaneously teaching the principles of living a *Godly* life with blessed assurance, above all abundant living, and in good health as recorded in Scripture. This parable is acknowledged and recorded biblically by four eyewitnesses; the Apostles *Matthew, Mark, Luke, and John*. Their testimonies are all consistent with regard to text and content. According to Scripture, we are admonished to **"Let every word be established by two or three witnesses"** *(2 Corinthians 13:1)*.

An exegesis of this Scripture reading would not be complete without first providing an "as written in the Bible" version of the parable. But before I present my case and study, I would like to preface this with a few things. First, I have decided to use only Mark's version of the parable as testimony, although as previously stated, all accounts are consistent on the details. Next, there is a **Sidebar** in this case that I feel must be presented first in order to help the reader to understand the overall intent of this *"Seed Time and Harvest"* concept, and how it relates to the act of shooting a Free-throw with precision.

It should be understood that after Jesus preached this sermon and He was alone with the twelve disciples, they asked Jesus to explain the parable. Jesus began to answer the question with a question. He said to the twelve, as I take the liberty of paraphrasing, *"You mean you really don't understand this parable"?* He continued by answering the question with a second question, *"How then will you know any other parable?"* But ask yourself what is the question not saying? As I use my own spiritual imagination; I interpret this to say if you **can** understand this parable then you will be able to understand all of the parables of Jesus teachings.

At that point, Jesus told the twelve, ***"Unto you, it is given to know the mystery of the kingdom of God: but unto them that are without, all these things are done in parables: that through the parables are revealed the mysteries of God. But to those who are without God, the parable will remain a mystery."*** It is only easy to understand by the believer, the unbeliever will not be able to logically receive the spiritual message. For the Scriptures teach that **He who worships God must worship Him in spirit and in truth.** He further states, if you, the reader and hearers of His word, can receive this concept and accept the principles taught, you will be able to understand and receive the rest of the literary treasures presented in the Bible. In short, it is my intent to show the reader how these **"Seed Time and Harvest"** principles, when faithfully applied in life, as well as in free-throws **works!** That being said, let's go into the Scriptures:

Luke 8:5-16
"A sower went out to sow his seed: and as he sowed, some fell by the way side; and it was trodden down, and the fowls of the air devoured it. And some fell upon a rock; and as soon as it was sprung up, it withered away, because it lacked moisture. And some fell among thorns; and the thorns sprang up with it, and choked it. And other fell on good ground, and sprang up, and bare fruit an hundredfold. And when he had said these things, he cried,

He that hath ears to hear, let him hear. And his disciples asked him, saying, What might this parable be?

"And he said, Unto you it is given to know the mysteries of the kingdom of God: but to others in parables; that seeing they might not see, and hearing they might not understand.

"Now the parable is this: The seed is the word of God. Those by the way side are they that hear; then cometh the devil, and taketh away the word out of their hearts, lest they should believe and be saved. They on the rock are they, which, when they hear, receive the word with joy; and these have no root, which for a while believe, and in time of temptation fall away. And that which fell among thorns are they, which, when they have heard, go forth, and are choked with cares and riches and pleasures of this life, and bring no fruit to perfection.

"But that on the good ground are they, which in an honest and good heart, having heard the word, keep it, and bring forth fruit with patience. No man, when he hath lighted a candle, covereth it with a vessel, or putteth it under a bed; but setteth it on a candlestick, that they which enter in may see the light."

Let me begin by giving you the setting. The sermon that you have just read has just ended. All of the many people have now gone, and Jesus was alone with the twelve disciples. Jesus began to give them his personal interpretation of the parable. He told them about a farmer who was in the fields planting seeds in his garden. However, He evidently was spreading the seed in a careless manner because the parable tells us that some seed fell on four different types of ground area.

There was the stony ground, there was the rocky ground, there was some that merely fell by the wayside and did not really get buried, and then there was the seed that fell on *good ground*. As I study this I think about the fact that this was no new thing with God. We can go as far back as Creation when God made the first man which was Adam; He has always wanted us to become fruit bearers. In fact, the very first location in Creation that God had made for man was in a garden (*Garden of Eden*).

He gave the first man the responsibility of maintaining this beautiful garden and he commanded him to be productive in all things. (Be Fruitful and to multiply) Personally, I don't believe God would tell the man to become something that He knows he is not capable of being. We must also understand that when Jesus speaks of the sower who sowed seed. It is not literal seed he is spreading but figuratively it is the word of God that he is commissioned to spread.

Just like in the natural, some of the seed would fall on four kinds of ground. Again, the soil would represent the various types of people, the heart of mankind. When we consider the fact that this is really the word that he is spreading and just like the seed, some of God's word will be received when heard, and Jesus said when we hear the word of the kingdom and we don't quite understand, Satan comes immediately and takes away that part that was received in their hearts.

This is the seed or word which was thrown off by the wayside. Then there were the people who received the word which fell in stony places. These are people who I believe have what the Bible describes as a *hardened heart*. Meaning, they will receive the word with joy, but there minds are already made up on the things of God and have in a while when the bills come in, struggles of life endure and life presents its natural challenges, they become discouraged and loose the faith.

Next, there is the person who receives the word on thorny ground. This person is the one who is deceived by the wealth and riches of this world. The Apostle Matthew said it like this; *they have their reward*, here on earth which implies they can expect no other rewards in the eternal afterlife from God. The word is then choked out and they can therefore not be fruitful or beneficial to the kingdom of God. Finally, there is the person who has received the word of God on good ground.

He has ears to hear the word of God and understands the mysteries of his kingdom. These people have been found faithful stewards to God and will produce much fruit. As a matter of fact, depending on his level of faith, some of these people will receive a hundred percent, some sixty, and some thirty percent more harvest in the spreading of God's word and will be entitled to become heirs to His royal kingdom; living life with more abundance. Then the question was asked by the Apostles to Jesus, *"Why do you speak these words in parables?"* As I interpret, Jesus told them the reason is God has given His word to be understood only by his followers. Children of perdition, or of Satan, will not be able to rationalize the parables. This is one of the reasons the Scriptures teach us *"It is impossible to please God without faith."* Additionally, this is the reason an all knowing God had given everyone what the Bible describes as the measure of faith. God knew we would need it and therefore provided or supplied our every need in this action.

Consequently, this third Scripture brings it own home when it says, **"the just shall live by faith."** This Scripture suggests faith as a way of life; which by nature of the game of basketball would include even the concept of shooting a basketball. Consider the thought of basketball as a way of life. As an experiment, I would like you to shoot your free throws with faith as the cornerstone. I would have you believe you will get the desired results by using your faith only; but you must remember *faith without works is dead faith*, according to the Bible (James 2:20). I am not suggesting dead faith as a way to success. This must include work, conditioning, and commitment to the way of life you have chosen.

Day 7 Drills and Exercises

Remember the suicides form the earlier chapter? Remember the team drills that require competition? This time we will combine the two. The only difference is we will incorporate the use of the basketball. Starting at one end of the court while dribbling the ball at full speed, you will run to the half court line then return and go full speed to the other end. Repeat procedure while alternating hands when you return.

> *"Experience is the best teacher... It is the only scenario where you get your test first and the lesson afterwards"*

—Coach Alex Gillum

Gillum-ISM's Quote Interpretation No.7

> *"In the game of basketball as well as in the game of life, we have to deal with an on-going process. Oftentimes, basketball is very improvisational. The point guard is identified as the coach on the floor, and while simultaneously setting up the play, he may need to simply take the ball straight to the hoop. Although, in the same exact play, he may choose the option of driving to the hoop and then shooting a quick pass to the open player in the corner. In either case, the experienced player is the most effective player. Based on his past experience, in most cases, he will make the right choice for the situation.*

—Coach Alex Gillum

CHAPTER 8

Three Seconds

There is only one key component that is consistent with both the game of life and the game on the court that governs us and in fact, we cannot control. This component is the element of time. In the Bible, the Book of Ecclesiastes speaks on this and teaches us that there is a time for everything. *"To every thing there is a season, and a time to every purpose under the heaven: a time to be born, and a time to die; a time to plant, and a time to pluck up that which is planted; a time to kill, and a time to heal; a time to break down, and a time to build up; a time to weep, and a time to laugh; a time to mourn, and a time to dance; a time to cast away stones, and a time to gather stones together; a time to embrace, and a time to refrain from embracing; a time to get, and a time to lose; a time to keep, and a time to cast away; a time to rend, and a time to sew; a time to keep silence, and a time to speak; a time to love, and a time to hate; a time of war, and a time of peace"* (Ecclesiastes 3:1-8). The fact is: our Creator has specifically allocated and designed the world in such a way that we as living beings would be assigned a time to live and to serve His kingdom.

Obviously, this was evidently an important and necessary element in the overall infrastructure. In fact, God describes this time factor as His gift to us. *"And also that every man should eat and drink, and enjoy the good of all his labour, it is the gift of God"* (Ecclesiastes 3:13). He concludes with this; *"I know that, whatsoever God doeth, it shall be for ever: nothing can be put to it, nor any thing taken from it: and God doeth it, that men should fear before him. ¹⁵ That which hath been is now; and that which is to be hath already been; and God requireth that which is past" (Ecclesiastes 3:14-15)*. In the game of basketball and life, I have learned that each and every second of the game should not be taken for granted. Those valuable moments may be ultimately just as important and can be the determining factor in the overall win or lose results. King Solomon, the author of the Book of Ecclesiastes is my first witness, according to Scripture.

I need at least one more witness: Consider the thief on the cross during the Crucifixion of Our Lord and Savior Jesus Christ. While hanging on the cross next too Jesus actually dying; with little time left to live; one of them took advantage of the little time left to live by speaking to Jesus and asking him to please remember him. *"And he said unto Jesus, Lord, remember me when thou comest into thy kingdom. ⁴³ And Jesus said unto him, Verily I say unto thee, Today shalt thou be with me in paradise"* (Luke 23:42-43).

In this chapter, I am compelled to share an experience regarding a time that still haunts me even to this very day. However, the only thing good about making an error is only when we learn something from the experience—right? It happened during my high school basketball season. At that time, I literally and figuratively lived the game of basketball. I mean, when I was not at practice, I would go home eat dinner and get right back out there on the court. I played pickup basketball games in the neighborhood, where I would usually win playing for a dollar a game. It was this particular day where I was in the zone! Do you know what I mean? I would eat, sleep, and drink the game! On game day, our coach would tell us to basically deprive ourselves of even touching the ball.

This was not really that easy for a guy who was so in love with even the touch of the ball. However, it did add a special passion to the shot on game day. On the last practice before the big tournament, I went to my coach and told him whatever you do make sure you play me this game! I added I have been shooting all week and I don't think I have missed a single shot! I don't think I could miss if I tried!

Here is where the game gets serious! I sat through the entire game watching every quarter, just waiting for my chance to enter the game. I knew I was going to be awesome! I would impress all of my teammates with my outstanding scoring ability and perhaps even be the players who would make the winning score! It was now the fourth quarter and there were only three seconds left on the clock, and I was so angry! I felt betrayed by my coach after I have confided in him secretly of my extreme confidence in my basketball skills. All of a sudden, I hear my name, "Johnny!" the coach shouted, then it was repeated by a few of my teammates. "Johnny!" he shouted again. I refused to move, I thought, what could I possibly do with 3 seconds left on the clock? I saw myself playing, if not all of the game most of the game and making an impact as a significant player for my team. I had all of the faith and confidence in myself that I truly believed there was absolutely no one on the court that could stop me or play the game better than me.

In hindsight, I did not feel it at the time, but I certainly felt the extreme error in my judgment later. I cannot tell you how many times I have visualized myself back there sitting on that same bench and thinking about the confidence my coach must have had in me to decide to call me at that critical point of the game. The strategic decision to place a player whom the other team had not seen perform the entire game, could have caused the other team to underestimate me and leave wide open with a greater opportunity to possibly score. It was a crucial decision and I made a selfish decision that could have possibly given me all of the glory and respect from my fellow teammates that I had craved without playing and scoring the entire game.

In that moment and time, in which I now believe was predestined for me to have the desires of my heart, as our Heavenly Father has promised. *"Delight thyself also in the LORD: and he*

shall give thee the desires of thine heart" *(Psalm 37:4).* Also, there was this word from the Lord... ***"Again I say unto you, that if two of you shall agree on earth as touching any thing that they shall ask, it shall be done for them of my Father which is in heaven"*** *(Matthew 18:19).* Little did I know, my coach and I were in spiritual agreement? According to the word of God, he believed as I did that I was the perfect person for that time to bring impact to the outcome of the game. Later, I realized that God wanted me to achieve my personal goal, and I just got in my own way. Essentially, we are capable as self-willed creatures of God to block our blessings! God describes us as not just conquerors, but in fact, he calls us more than conquerors! ***"Nay, in all these things we are more than conquerors through him that loved us"*** *(Romans 8:37).*

How many times have we made this mistake in life? That job promotion that you worked so hard to earn, that first house that or car that you wanted, that college degree that you had worked and studied so hard to achieve. It was opportunities like these throughout my life that I have always brought back to that same old bench and that chosen time. I would think, I could have met my goal in those final three seconds. Instead of listening to that voice of my inner Holy Spirit, I listened to that unholy voice of the deceiver who had me thinking my coach did not believe in me enough, and he did I not have the confidence in me. I did not even consider that fact that I was specifically selected to be the one guy on the team for that particular time to enter and take that final shot that I knew and had told my coach that I absolutely could not possibly miss.

I was prepared for the task, but not willing to respect the decision my coach had made to use me at the time that he needed me the most. We lost the game and I lost the chance that I had worked so hard to achieve. Now, let's consider that thief hanging on the cross next to Jesus, what if he had thought I have been a robber all of my life, I deserve to die!

How can I ask the Son of God to even think about a sinner like me? He had those same three seconds and, little did he know his decision to speak to Jesus at that particular time was, in fact, a Soul Saving and crucial decision. Remember, there were two thieves hanging on the cross. They both had the same opportunity, but the one who stepped out on faith would win his soul and be accepted into the Kingdom of God. In the days and times that I am often reminded of this experience, I take this Scripture as a teaching tool and I feel that I am spiritually led to take this opportunity to share it with you.

Joshua 1:9
"Have not I commanded thee? Be strong and of a good courage; be not afraid, neither be thou dismayed: for the LORD thy God is with thee whithersoever thou goest."

CHAPTER 9

Diligently

Diligently (dil·i·gent·ly ˈdiləjəntlē), is an adverb. Defined, diligently means to show care and conscientiousness in one's work or duties. I challenge you to take your faith to the next level by simply being diligent. In this chapter, we will explore the cause and effect results of a lifestyle with diligence when we pursue our passions in the game of basketball and life. The Scripture references in this chapter are presented as an illustration and confirmation to the rewards for the living as well as the opportunity to obtain the incorruptible crowns of God. Meditate on them daily. My challenge to the reader is to administer the same passion and diligence in basketball. Seek to be your very best, and you will enjoy the rewards of your success!

Crowns of God

The verses of Scripture mentioned in this chapter will help you recognize and live under the many crowns of God according to faith. Your diligence must be founded on your faith in God; it is the only way you can please God. The Bible expressly says, **"Without faith it is impossible to please him: for he that cometh to God must believe that he is, and that he is a rewarder of them that diligently seek him"** (Hebrews: 11:6).

Our God wears many crowns and He also rejects many crowns. I believe God's will is that we also wear many crowns. I have listed here many of God's crowns. It is my prayer that you learn to wear the crowns that God approves and reject those that he disapproves.

Crown of Knowledge

"He that diligently seeketh good procureth favour: but he that seeketh mischief, it shall come unto him" (Proverbs: 11:27).

"The simple inherit folly: but the prudent are crowned with knowledge" (Proverbs 14:18).

"And ye shall seek me, and find me, when ye shall search for me with all your heart" (Jeremiah 29:13).

Crown of Life

"Blessed is the man that endureth temptation: for when he is tried, he shall receive the crown of life, which the Lord hath promised to them that love him" (James 1:12).

"Fear none of those things which thou shalt suffer: behold, the devil shall cast some of you into prison, that ye may be tried; and ye shall have tribulation ten days: be thou faithful unto death, and I will give thee a crown of life" (Revelations 2:10).

"And every man that striveth for the mastery is temperate in all things. Now they do it to obtain a corruptible crown; but we an incorruptible" (1 Corinthians 9:25).

"Behold, I come quickly: hold that fast which thou hast, that no man take thy crown" (Revelations 3:11).

Crown of Rejoicing

"Therefore, by brethren dearly beloved and longed for, my joy and crown, so stand fast in the Lord, my dearly beloved" (Philippians 4:1).

"For what is our hope, or joy, or crown of rejoicing? Are not even ye in the presence of our Lord Jesus Christ at his coming?" (1 Thessalonians 2:19)

Crown of Righteousness

*"Henceforth there is laid up for me a **crown of righteousness**, which the Lord, the righteous judge, shall give me at that day: and not to me only, but unto all them also that love his appearing"* (2 Timothy 4:8).

Crown of Glory and Honour (The crown of Jesus)

*"But we see Jesus, who was made a little lower than the angels for the suffering of death, **crowned with glory and honour**; that he by the grace of God should taste death for every man"* (Hebrews 2:9).

*"And there appeared a great wonder in heaven; a woman clothed with the sun, and the moon under her feet, and upon her head a **crown of twelve stars**"* (Revelation 12:1).

*"Thou shalt also be a **crown of glory** in the hand of the LORD, and a royal diadem in the hand of thy God"* **(Isaiah 62:3)**.

*"And when the chief Shepherd shall appear, ye shall receive a **crown of glory that fadeth not away**"* (Peter 5:4).

Crown of the Conqueror

*"And I saw, and behold a white horse: and he that sat on him had a bow; and **a crown was given unto him**: and he went forth **conquering, and to conquer**"* (Revelations 6:2).

Crown of Wisdom

"The **crown of the wise** is their riches: but the foolishness of fools is folly" *(Proverbs 14:24).*

"For riches are not for ever: and doth the crown endure to every generation" *(Proverbs 27:24)?*

Crown of Lovingkindness and Mercy

"Who redeemeth thy life from destruction; who **crowneth thee with lovingkindness and tender mercies**" *(Psalms 103:3-5).*

Crown of Pride (You do not want to receive)

"Woe to the **crown of pride**, to the drunkards of Ephraim, whose glorious beauty is a fading flower, which are on the head of the fat valleys of them that are overcome with wine" *(Isaiah 28:1)!*

"The **crown of pride**, the drunkards of Ephraim, shall be trodden under feet" *(Isaiah 28:3).*

Crown of Old Men

"Children's children are the **crown of old men**; and the glory of children are their fathers" *(Proverbs 17:6).*

"A virtuous woman is a crown to her husband: but she that maketh ashamed is as rottenness in his bones" *(Proverbs 12:4).*

crown of the anointing oil of God

"Neither shall he go out of the sanctuary, nor profane the sanctuary of his God; for **the crown of the anointing oil** of his God is upon him: I am the LORD" *(Leviticus 21:12).*

Crown of Thorns (You do not want to receive)

"Then came Jesus forth, wearing the **crown of thorns**, and the purple robe. And Pilate saith unto them, Behold the man" (John 19:5)!

Diligently Seeking the Kingdom:

"But take **diligent heed to do the commandment and the law**, which Moses the servant of the LORD charged you, to love the LORD your God, and to walk in all his ways, and to keep his commandments, and to cleave unto him, and to serve him with all your heart and with all your soul" (Joshua 22:5).

"And it shall come to pass, if thou shalt hearken **diligently** unto the voice of the LORD thy God, to observe and to do all his commandments which I command thee this day, that the LORD thy God will set thee on high above all nations of the earth" (Deuteronomy 28:1).

"For if ye shall **diligently** keep all these commandments which I command you, to do them, to love the LORD your God, to walk in all his ways, and to cleave unto him; Then will the LORD drive out all these nations from before you, and ye shall possess greater nations and mightier than yourselves" (Deuteronomy 11:22-23).

"Thou hast commanded us to keep thy precepts **diligently**" (Psalms 119:4).

"Ask, and it shall be given you; seek, and ye shall find; knock, and it shall be opened unto you: For every one that asketh receiveth; and he that seeketh findeth; and to him that knocketh it shall be opened" (Matthew 7:6-8).

"Therefore came I forth to meet thee, **diligently** to seek thy face, and I have found thee" (Proverbs 7:15).

"He becometh poor that dealeth with a slack hand: but the hand of the **diligent** maketh rich" (Proverbs 10:4).

"Only take heed to thyself, and keep thy soul **diligently**, lest thou forget the things which thine eyes have seen, and lest they depart from thy heart all the days of thy life: but teach them thy sons, and thy sons' sons" (Deuteronomy 4:9).

"Ye shall **diligently** keep the commandments of the LORD your God, and his testimonies, and his statutes, which he hath commanded thee" (Deuteronomy 6:17).

"Hear **diligently** my speech, and let this be your consolations" (Job 21:2).

"Hear **diligently** my speech, and my declaration with your ears" (Job 13:17).

"Receiving the end of your faith, even the salvation of your souls. Of which salvation the prophets have enquired and searched **diligently** who prophesied of the grace that should come unto you: Searching what, or what manner of time the Spirit of Christ which was in them did signify when it testified beforehand the sufferings of Christ, and the glory that should follow" (1 Peter 1:9-11).

"Wherefore, beloved, seeing that ye look for such things, be **diligent** that ye may be found of him in peace, without spot, and blameless" (2 Peter 3:14).

"The soul of the sluggard desireth, and hath nothing: but the soul of the **diligent** shall be made fat" (Proverbs 13:4).

"The thoughts of the **diligent** tend only to plenteousness; but of every one that is hasty only to want" (Proverbs 21:5).

"Seest thou a man **diligent** in his business? He shall stand before kings; he shall not stand before mean men" (Proverbs 22:29).

"Whatsoever is commanded by the God of heaven, let it be **diligently** done for the house of the God of heaven: for why should there be wrath against the realm of the king and his sons?" (Ezra 7:23)

"Wherefore do ye spend money for that which is not bread? and your labour for that which satisfieth not? hearken diligently unto me, and eat ye that which is good, and let your soul delight itself in fatness" (Isaiah 55:2).

"Let us hear the conclusion of the whole matter: Fear God, and keep his commandments: for this is the whole duty of man" (Ecclesiastes 12:13).

According to Scripture, we can see that God is the great giver and rewarder of those who will diligently seek him. This is our personal covenant that God has declared over all of our lives as believers. The questions are not whether or not you believe and accept God as your spiritual source, but:

1. Are you **DILIGENTLY** seeking his face?
2. Do you want to receive your rewards from the Creator?
3. Are you regularly listening to the word of God?
4. How many **CROWNS** do you seek to receive from God?
5. Are you aware that diligently seeking the word of God is a **COMMANDMENT** and not merely a suggestion?

6. Did you know that when you obey the commandment of diligently seeking God, you are actually receiving the end of your faith and the salvation of your soul?
7. Do you teach your children and your grandchildren the importance of diligently seeking the word of God as he has commanded you to do?
8. Are you getting fat on the word of God?

Summary

The act of shooting a free throw is fundamentally simple. It does not require very much physical strength to pick up a basketball, aim it at the basket and take a shot. In fact, one could say it is as easy as reaching out to receive a free gift. According to Scripture, Jesus Christ is the free gift from God to the Saints, which is the believer. The common denominator seems to be both scenarios appear to be easy to obtain, yet so many of us, unfortunately, will miss the opportunity.

"But not as the offence, so also is the free gift. For if through the offence of one many be dead, much more the grace of God, and the gift by grace, which is by one man, Jesus Christ, hath abounded unto many" (Romans 5:15).

Today, in America we live in a complicated world. The second term of the USA's first African American President who has sanctioned the legalization of Gay marriages, he is pro-Abortion, and the first sitting President who chose not to acknowledge National Prayer Day. Meanwhile, simultaneously only this year after a young kid goes into a church with a machine gun, shoots and kills several people do they finally decide to take the rebel flag down in South Carolina which has flown in the state since the Civil War. This Just In "The Donald", that is Donald Trump shocks America as he announces his candidacy for President and the fact that his campaign will be running on the "I AM NOT A POLITICIAN" banner.

He is currently the leader in all polls to date. Finally, there is Cecil the Lion who was recently shot and killed in Africa by a local dentist who paid $50,000 dollars for the opportunity.

This incident is sad, and certainly, I am sympathetic for the loss of a dying breed; but come on America, get your priorities straight! How can we justify criticizing this man for shooting a lion in Africa then raise over $300,000 dollars in support of this cause while police are shooting and killing America's kids in Ferguson, Missouri, in Chicago, Illinois, in New Orleans, LA, in Dallas, TX in epidemic proportion and I have never heard of anyone raising any level of substantial money for the families of these our slain children.

You can't even go to a movie theater today without worrying about someone next to you who may have a bomb, pepper spray, and an assault weapon under cover. Stop the World I want to get off!

Romans 5:18-19
"Therefore as by the offence of one judgment came upon all men to condemnation; even so by the righteousness of one the free gift came upon all men unto justification of life. [19] For as by one man's disobedience many were made sinners, so by the obedience of one shall many be made righteous.

In this book and the Bible, you may have noticed the word "fruit" is often used metaphorically. Throughout the Scriptures, God implies and even emphasizes the fact that He wants all of his children to aspire to be like a good farmer who plants seeds in expectants of a great harvest. We are admonished to be good fruit bearers for the Lord. The metaphor is an exemplary rendition of what many describe as the great gift of salvation that God has provided by allowing His only begotten son *Jesus Christ* to be a living sacrifice for all of our sins.

I suppose the next obvious question would be how does all of this relate to the concept of shooting a free throw accurately and effectively? I challenge each reader to consider the basketball as your seed and each shot that you make as the fruit. The more baskets made the more fruit!

In conclusion, I have prepared a "Top 12" list of biblical free gifts that were comprised for your perusal. I would like to preface this section first by explaining a few disclaimers. The decision to feature 12 of these gifts was based on the fact that Jesus selected 12 disciples to follow him and witness, minister, and edify the body of Christ by converting the lost and delivering them from the sin nature which was allowed to enter this world through the disobedience of the first Adam. Clearly, there are more that twelve gifts that were given to us by the Creator. My Top 12 List was a personal choice that realistically could have gone on for quite awhile. In preparing this list, I just kept on thinking of even more that should be listed. Such as the free gift of the believer to have "free will." God could have made us like robots and we would simply be programmed to do whatever he had designed us to do. There is the free gift of prayer. We can go to the throne of God with our petitions and as long as the prayers are according to His will; they will be answered and delivered. God has given us the power to get wealth; "But thou shalt remember the Lord thy God: for it is he that giveth thee **power to get wealth**, that he may establish his covenant which he sware unto thy fathers, as it is this day." We must remember we are talking about the Great Giver. The Most High God, Jehovah. In the words of the old time preacher; "**You Just Can't Beat God Giving!**" Finally, I would just like to emphasize the Spiritual Gifts that God has given to each and everyone of us. This gift is so very important and should not be taken for granted. If you do not know what your spiritual gift is. I encourage you to study the book of Corinthians and read over and over allowing the Holy Spirit to speak into your life. According to the book of Joshua; *"This book of the law shall not depart out of thy mouth; but thou shalt meditate therein day and night, that thou mayest observe to do according to all that is written therein: for then thou shalt make thy way prosperous, and then thou* *shalt have good success." Then He continued; "Have not I commanded thee? Be strong and of a good courage; be not afraid, neither be thou dismayed: for the Lord thy God is with thee whithersoever thou goest"* (Joshua 1:8-9).

Top 12 Spiritual Gifts Freely Given by God

1. *Fruits of the Spirit. (Love, Joy, Peace...) reference Scripture Galatians 5:22-23* But the fruit of the Spirit is love, joy, peace, longsuffering, gentleness, goodness, faith, Meekness, temperance: against such, there is no law.
2. *The Measure of Faith.* For I say, through the grace given unto me, to every man that is among you, not to think of himself more highly than he ought to think; but to think soberly, according as God hath dealt to every man the measure of faith (Romans 12:3).
3. *New Mercy Every Morning.* It is of the Lord's mercies that we are not consumed because his compassions fail not. They are new every morning: great is thy faithfulness (Lamentations 3:22-24).
4. The Comforter (*Holy Spirit*). But the Comforter, which is the Holy Ghost, whom the Father will send in my name, he shall teach you all things, and bring all things to your remembrance, whatsoever I have said unto you (John 14:6).
5. The Free Gift of Grace and Salvation. But not as the offence, so also is the free gift. For if through the offence of one many be dead, much more the grace of God, and the gift by grace, which is by one man, Jesus Christ, hath abounded unto many (Romans 5:15).
6. The Declaration by God to be identified as the Righteousness of God. To declare, I say, at this time his

righteousness: that he might be just, and the justifier of him which believeth in Jesus (Romans 3:26).
7. Your Living Body is God's Gift. What? know ye not that your body is the temple of the Holy Ghost which is in you, which ye have of God, and ye are not your own? For ye are bought with a price: therefore glorify God in your body, and in your spirit, which are God's (I Corinthians 6:19-20).
8. The Ministry of Reconciliation. And all things are of God, who hath reconciled us to himself by Jesus Christ, and hath given to us the ministry of reconciliation (2 Corinthians 5:17-19).
9. The Word of God. For the word of God is quick, and powerful, and sharper than any two edged sword, piercing even to the dividing asunder of soul and spirit, and of the joints and marrow, and is a discerner of the thoughts and intents of the heart (Hebrews 4:12).
10. Power to Heal against unclean spirits and against sickness and all diseases. And when he had called unto him his twelve disciples, he gave them power against unclean spirits, to cast them out, and to heal all manner of sickness and all manner of disease (Matthew 10:1-3).
11. Spiritual Gifts. But the manifestation of the Spirit is given to every man to profit withal. For to one is given by the Spirit the word of wisdom; to another the word of knowledge by the same Spirit; [9] To another faith by the same Spirit; to another the gifts of healing by the same Spirit; [10] To another the working of miracles; to another prophecy; to another discerning of spirits; to another divers kinds of tongues; to another the interpretation of tongues: [11] But all these worketh that one and the selfsame Spirit, dividing to every man severally as he will (1 Corinthians 12:7-11).
12. Freedom from sin. If the Son therefore shall make you free, ye shall be free indeed (John 8:36).

Invitation to Christian Discipleship and Ambassadorship

In the Old Testament of God's final will; we discover the recorded history, genealogy, and Holy Spirit power in the name as the book cohesively reveal the Promise and/or Covenant with the true and living God of the New Testament. By accepting this cordial invitation to Christian discipleship, you have been changed! You must now begin to see yourself the same way God see's you... *We are Ambassador's for Christ! (2 Cor. 5:20)*

Salvation is God's greatest gift to you. "The gift of God is eternal life through Jesus Christ our Lord" (Romans 6:23). When someone offers you a priceless gift, the wisest thing you can do is accept it! This very moment, you can receive Christ's gift of salvation by sincerely praying this simple prayer from your heart:

Dear God, I know that I am a sinner. I know that you love me and want to save me. Jesus, I believe You are the Son of God, who died on the cross to pay for my sins. I believe God raised You from the dead. I now turn from my sin and, by faith, receive You as my personal Lord and Savior. Come into my heart, forgive my sins, and save me, Lord Jesus. In Your name I pray. Amen.

CREDITS

Jodi Grimes: Editing

Eric Dunbar: Cover design and formatting

NOTES

Made in the USA
Columbia, SC
27 February 2025

bd2ede88-f05e-4325-9302-519062fe612eR01